Management and Business Skills in the Built Environment

THE BUILT ENVIRONMENT SERIES OF TEXTBOOKS (BEST)

Executive Editor: Professor Tony Collier, Dean, Faculty of the Built Environment, University of Central England, Birmingham, UK

Co-ordinating Editor: David Burns, Faculty of the Built Environment, University of Central England, Birmingham, UK

Assistant Editor: Jean Baron, Faculty of the Built Environment, University of Central England, Birmingham, UK

ADVISORY BOARD:

James Armstrong *Visiting Professor, Faculty of Technology, Kingston University*

David Cormican *Deputy Director, North West Institute of Further and Higher Education*

Bryan Jefferson *Architectural Advisor to the Secretary of State, Department of National Heritage*
Visiting Professor, Sheffield University, Faculty of Architectural Studies

Howard Land *Professional Training Consultant, RICS*

Alan Osborne *Chairman, Tarmac Construction Ltd*
Chairman, Construction Industry Standing Conference (CISC)

John Tarn *Roscoe Professor of Architecture, University of Liverpool*

Alan Wenban-Smith *Assistant Director of Planning and Architecture, Birmingham City Council*

This series of textbooks responds to changes that are occurring throughout the construction industry and in further education. It focuses on aspects of the curriculum that are common to all professions in the built environment. The principal aim of BEST is to provide texts that are relevant to more than one course and the texts therefore address areas of commonality in an original and innovative way. Learning aids in the texts such as chapter objectives, checklists, and workpieces will appeal to all students.

OTHER TITLES IN THE SERIES

Collaborative Practice in the Built Environment

Design, Technology and the Development Process in the Built Environment

Forthcoming

Law and the Built Environment

Buildings, Neighbourhoods and Places

Environmental Issues in the Built Environment

International Trends in the Construction Industry

Economics and the Built Environment

MANAGEMENT AND BUSINESS SKILLS IN THE BUILT ENVIRONMENT

EDITED BY MIKE WATERHOUSE AND GEOFF CROOK
Faculty of the Built Environment, University of Central England, Birmingham, UK

E & FN SPON
An Imprint of Chapman & Hall

London · Glasgow · Weinheim · New York · Tokyo · Melbourne · Madras

Published by E & FN Spon, an imprint of Chapman & Hall,
2–6 Boundary Row, London SE1 8HN, UK

Chapman & Hall, 2–6 Boundary Row, London SE1 8HN, UK

Blackie Academic & Professional, Wester Cleddens Road, Bishopbriggs, Glasgow G64 2NZ, UK

Chapman & Hall GmbH, Pappelallee 3, 69469 Weinheim, Germany

Chapman & Hall USA, 115 Fifth Avenue, New York NY 10003, USA

Chapman & Hall Japan, ITP-Japan, Kyowa Building, 3F, 2-2-1 Hirakawacho, Chiyoda-ku, Tokyo 102, Japan

Chapman & Hall Australia, Thomas Nelson Australia, 102 Dodds Street, South Melbourne, Victoria 3205, Australia

Chapman & Hall India, R. Seshadri, 32 Second Main Road, CIT East, Madras 600 035, India

First edition 1995

© 1995 E & FN Spon

Typeset in 10/12pt Caslon by Saxon Graphics Ltd, Derby

Printed in Great Britain by the Alden Press, Osney Mead, Oxford

ISBN 0 419 19540 8

A catalogue record for this book is available from the British Library

Library of Congress Catalog Card Number: 95-67589

∞ Printed on permanent acid-free text paper, manufactured in accordance with ANSI/NISO Z39.48-1992 and ANSI/NISO Z39.48-1984 (Permanence of Paper).

CONTENTS

CONTENTS

CONTRIBUTORS

John Brunsdon
Consultant in Management
    Education
Business School
University of Central England
Birmingham

Geoff Crook
Principal Lecturer
Faculty of Built Environment
University of Central England
Birmingham

Graham Darbyshire
Principal
GMD Associates
Birmingham

Diana Eastcott
Deputy Head of Learning
    Methods Unit
University of Central England
Birmingham

Bob Farmer
Head of Learning Methods Unit
University of Central England
Birmingham

Barry Hampson
Financial Consultant
Milton Keynes

Anne Hill
Senior Lecturer
Faculty of the Built Environment
University of Central England
Birmingham

Tash Khan
Personnel and Training Manager
Wimpey Construction plc

Mike Waterhouse
Senior Lecturer
Faculty of Built Environment
University of Central England
Birmingham

INTRODUCTION

This book is aimed at students and professionals in the built environment who wish to develop their management and business skills. If we are to thrive in the rapidly changing world in which we live, we may need the skills and knowledge to intervene and to stake a greater control over our own development.

This book is designed to help you to reflect upon your learning, to explore ways of learning and to make plans for your own personal growth and development.

To enable you to do this the book is organized around three themes:

- Chapters 1, 2 and 3: Learning how to manage yourself.
- Chapters 4, 5 and 6: Learning how to build and work in teams.
- Chapters 7, 8, 9 and 10 : Learning about the principal areas of business management.

Each of these themes is illustrated by examples and workpieces drawn from the built environment. Checklists are provided in each chapter to help you to reflect on your level of knowledge and understanding of this subject.

Management and Business Skills is aimed primarily at first year (level 1) undergraduates. However, we are aware that the various professions involved with the built environment have different requirements for management education and training. The book may well be more relevant to the upper levels of some courses leading to professional qualifications but our belief is that built environment professionals could benefit from improved business and management skills. Consequently undergraduate courses should embrace this material in their first year of study (level 1). In addition BTEC built environment and other courses may also find all or parts of the book relevant.

The overall aim of this book is to encourage aspiring built environment professionals and managers to evaluate their knowledge, skills and personal qualities and to develop strategies for their continuing development.

PART ONE

LEARNING HOW TO MANAGE YOURSELF

MANAGERS AND PROFESSIONALS

CHAPTER ONE

GEOFF CROOK AND MIKE WATERHOUSE

Professionals in the built environment perform a wide range of management roles. Does this mean that professionals are managers? This chapter explores the meanings of 'manager' and 'professional', drawing on examples from built environment practice.

After reading this chapter you should be able to:

● describe what is meant by professions and professionals in the built environment;

● describe what is meant by management activities, including task and process;

● describe the roles of a manager;

● discuss management functions in an organization;

● discuss the relationships between professionals and managers;

● explore why professionals might need to develop management and business skills.

A traditional view of a professional would be one of a specialist with technical expertise. Someone who acts professionally, or exhibits professionalism, is perceived as having a body of technical knowledge with skills and expertise in a particular area. This view of a professional is also likely to include the idea of membership of a professional body to which entry is determined by achieving approved qualifications and is maintained by adhering to certain standards.

WORKPIECE 1.1

SPECIALIST KNOWLEDGE AND EXPERTISE

Take a profession in which you have a particular interest and investigate its areas of specialist knowledge and expertise.

Try to identify those areas of technical knowledge and skills which a professional in this field would need to have competence.

(Hint: One of the easiest ways of doing this is to look at the syllabus of a course programme which has been approved by a professional body.)

PROFESSIONAL VALUES, STANDARDS AND CODES OF CONDUCT

Professionals spend many years in both studying for qualifications and gaining experience before being accepted as competent by a professional body. Sociologists have argued that as most professionals will spend much of their working lives with others who have had similar training and experiences, there is a tendency for them to adopt similar values, attitudes and norms.[1] Furthermore there may be an element of self reinforcement in the way individuals choose to follow a particular profession, influenced perhaps by their perception of the values that it holds. For example, it may be that the planning and housing professions have a particular attraction to those who put a high value on such principles as equality and equity.

Professional bodies define standards and set down codes of practice to guide and control the conduct of their members. Professionals can face difficult dilemmas where the wishes of a client, or of an employer, appear to be in conflict with their role as a professional – for example, a manager of a construction project may have to cope with a reduction in the budget for a scheme. The professionals in a project team may find great difficulty in reconciling their professional principles and standards with a request to modify the overall quality of a scheme. Codes of practice and the syllabus of approved educational programmes provide useful insights into the way each profession sees its role in society and its role in relation to that of other built environment professions.

BUILT ENVIRONMENT PROFESSIONS

A central feature of current practice in the built environment is the multiplicity of professional bodies and the often complex relationships between them. Four professions which are involved in a wide range of built environment activity are:

- architects
- engineers
- surveyors
- town planners.

These can be broken down into more specialist areas and other professional groups added:

- landscape architects
- urban designers
- building surveyors
- quantity surveyors
- estate managers
- housing managers
- project managers
- highway engineers
- structural engineers
- civil engineers.

Muir and Rance[2] argue for the improvement of collaborative working between these professional groups. They see the dangers of duplication and demarcation in the proliferation of built environment professions, with their own culture, standards and codes of practice and defining for themselves legitimate fields of activity.

Many professionals who have recently qualified in built environment disciplines may consider that they have little management knowledge and experience and identify this as a barrier to their future career development. Some perhaps do not yet see themselves as managers because they either do not have the title of 'manager', or do not manage other people, or do not have control over budgets. It often comes as a pleasant surprise for such professionals to discover that managers play much wider roles than they had first imagined and that they themselves already have a wide range of management skills, qualities and experience. Having this wider perspective is useful because it provides a basis for assessing strengths and weaknesses in management terms and for thinking through potential steps to personal development. It is also helpful in circumstances where it is necessary to articulate and sell

**LEARNING ABOUT
MANAGEMENT**

those management skills and experiences, such as in tendering for work or preparing a job application.

WHAT DO WE MEAN BY MANAGEMENT AND MANAGERS?

When we think about management, what images come to mind? Who are the managers and what do they do? Why are some people given the title of manager and others not? Don't read on any further until you have done Workpiece 1.2.

WORKPIECE 1.2

YOU AS A MANAGER

Think of circumstances in the past where you have acted as a manager.

Your examples might have included:

- selecting a course of study;
- deciding whether it would be cheaper to maintain your old car or to replace it with another;
- organizing and preparing for a holiday.

If you have been a captain of a sports team you may have been able to find examples fairly quickly. As a captain you might have been involved not only in deciding who will play in the team and what role they are to play, perhaps, but also in planning the strategy and encouraging members to play together as a team.

Look back at your list and see if you could improve it further. This workpiece should serve to illustrate that most people 'manage' for some of the time whether this be in the environment of their work, home or social lives. The idea of a manager sitting in an office spending most of the day taking key decisions on who does what and on how resources are to be allocated is a limited view. Much of the management activity comprises the more mundane clearing up of messes and simply getting things done. Management in one sense means coping – coping with the inadequacies of:

- resources
- information
- time
- preparation
- colleagues
- self.

Managers get things done; they complete tasks themselves or create and maintain an environment where others can work effectively on tasks. In doing so they spend much of their time planning and organizing how things are to be done, setting up ways of working and ensuring that they are effective. This planning, organizing and controlling of the ways things can be done, or of the processes for completing tasks, is one of the hallmarks of management activity.

Within management literature there have been many descriptions of these activities. The main management activities are listed below.[3]

PLANNING   The development of long and short range plans which may require the formulation of goals, objectives, strategies, policies, procedures and standards. It may also involve the perception and analysis of opportunities, problems and alternative courses of action and the design of programmes to achieve selected objectives.

ORGANIZING   The development of structures within which individuals and groups can work; assigning and coordinating activities by delegating authority, offering responsibility and requiring accountability.

STAFFING   The selection, training and assignment of personnel to specific organizational activities.

DIRECTING   The leadership of the organization through communication and motivation of organizational activities.

CONTROLLING   Observing and measuring organizational performance and environmental activities and, where necessary, modifying the plans and activities of the organization.

Within an organization, managers may be involved to differing extents in these activities. Figure 1.1 shows an organization with three levels of management hierarchy: top management, middle management and supervisory (or first line) management.[4] This example shows supervisory managers spending a great deal of time leading, motivating and controlling. The higher level managers are shown as spending a greater part of their time interpreting, planning and organizing.

So far the discussion of the meanings of 'management' and of 'what managers do' has been limited to the nature of the activities in which managers become involved. A further way of gaining insight into these

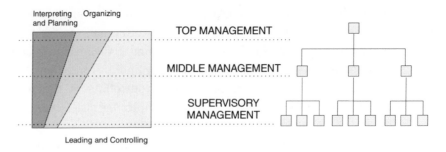

Figure 1.1 Management activities and levels of management.

meanings is to explore the roles that managers play. Managers are rather like actors in that they may need to adopt specific roles to manage in a particular circumstance. For example, a manager may have to act from time to time as the 'leader' of a group to help it to achieve its tasks successfully.

Many authors have discussed the kinds of role that managers may need to play.[5] They are often shown as falling into three broad groups: interpersonal, information and task implementation roles. **Interpersonal roles** typically involve communicating with other individuals and managing relationships within, or between, groups of people. Acting as a figure-head or as group leader or in a liaison role would also fall into this category. **Information roles** involve the collection and sharing of information both within an organization and between members of a group. They may also involve representing the views of a group to the outside world. The most commonly identified information roles are the spokesperson, the information seeker and disseminator. **Task implementation** roles involve deciding what needs to be done and how it should be done. These roles include the problem solver, delegator, negotiator, decision maker and resource allocator.

In addition to these there are a number of roles that managers may have to perform in relation to their staff, including: appraising performance; advising or counselling; supporting training and development. These roles are discussed in detail in Chapters 9 and 10.

MANAGERS IN ORGANIZATIONS

Managers are rarely free agents with complete discretion. They tend to act as agents for others. Managers are constrained and even conditioned by the structure, style, values and culture of the organization within which they work.

Whilst management is a generalist activity, in a large organization there may be a high degree of specialization with managers appointed to perform certain specialist, functional roles. For example, a large building company may employ a project manager, personnel manager, contracts manager, sales manager, public relations officer and so on. On the other hand, the principal in a small consultancy or practice may have to take responsibility for all of these functions and perform a wide range of management roles.

We have already said that most people manage for some of their time, whether this be in the environment of their work, home or social lives. With tasks such the design of a building, a structure or a landscape, there is clearly a need for specialist skills and expertise. However, there will inevitably be different ways of working towards the achievement of such tasks. Whilst those involved may all be professionals, the planning, organizing, controlling and monitoring of the processes are all management activities. Although professionals are essentially specialists operating within specific fields of work, they also perform management roles.

    In an organization, whether or not an individual is given the title of manager usually depends upon the proportion of time they are involved in management activities. Professionals therefore manage and are sometimes called managers, depending upon the extent to which they perform management roles and tasks.

Managers at each level in an organizational hierarchy may need a different mix of skills. Katz and Khan[6] describe the distribution of three types of management skill in organizations: conceptual, human and technical.

    Figure 1.2 shows technical skills as being of greatest importance at the supervisory level. Human skills are also important at this level in

PROFESSIONALS AS MANAGERS

MANAGEMENT DEVELOPMENT AND THE SPECIALIST PROFESSIONAL

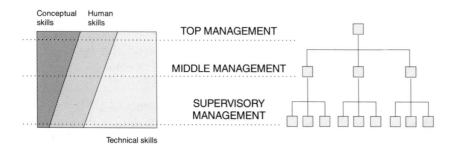

Figure 1.2 Management skills in an organizational hierarchy.

the frequent interaction with subordinates. Conceptual skills, however, may not be essential for all first-line supervisors. At the middle management level the need for technical skills decreases, human skills are still essential and conceptual skills gain in importance. At the top management level, where conceptual and human skills are particularly valuable, there may be relatively little need for technical expertise. It is assumed that chief executives in large companies can utilize the technical abilities of their subordinates. In smaller firms, however, technical expertise may still be important at the highest management level.[4]

Figure 1.2 helps to explain why promotion to the highest levels in an organization may often depend less upon the depth of specialist technical skills and more upon breadth or balance of technical, human and conceptual skills. For the professional who wishes to play a greater part in the management of the business, it is therefore important to gain broader experience and to develop the conceptual skills needed in seeing the wider picture. For senior managers in construction and development it is becoming increasingly important to be able to manage complex projects involving different technical disciplines.

Membership of a professional body often brings with it promotion, financial reward and status. For many of those who wish to climb yet further up the organizational ladder, however, there is the difficult dilemma of leaving behind their hard won technical skills and expertise, and spending an increasing proportion of their time performing management roles.

DEVELOPING MANAGEMENT SKILLS

The starting point for making personal development is self-knowledge. The key is to have an understanding of where you are now, a vision of where you want to be, and a perspective of the ways of getting there.[7] It is helpful therefore to be able to identify any blockages that may lie in your path. By identifying personal blockages it is possible to plan to address them. Assessing strengths and weaknesses in management terms is a positive first step in planning to improve effectiveness as a manager.

Figure 1.3 provides a guide to how chapters in this book may be used to develop further the skills and qualities of a manager.

SUMMARY

Professionals are specialists with technical expertise and skills in specific areas. A central feature of current practice in the built environment is the multiplicity of professional bodies and the often complex relationships between them. Recruitment, training, traditional patterns of working, standards and codes of conduct all contribute to the tendency

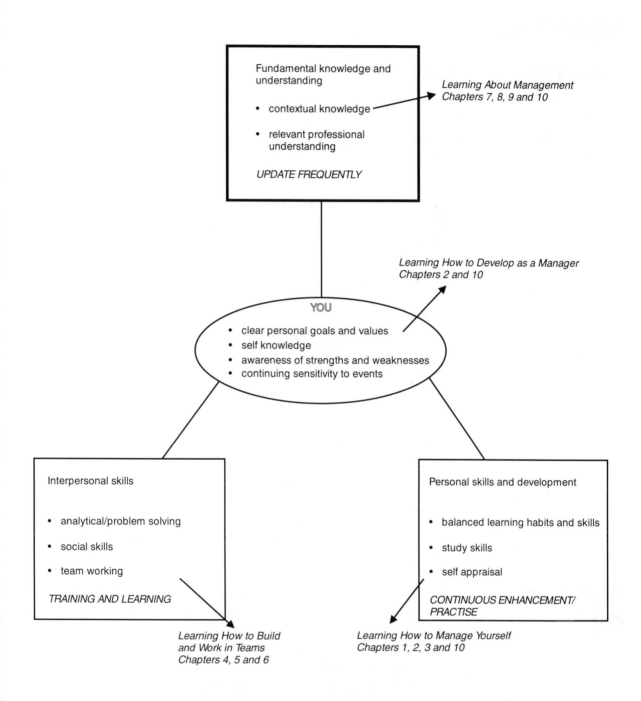

Figure 1.3 Developing management and business skills.

WORKPIECE 1.3

MAKING THIS BOOK WORK FOR YOU

Consider Figure 1.3 (Developing management and business skills).

● Scan the checklists at the end of each chapter in this book.

● Make a list for yourself of those areas of knowledge and skills which you feel you need to know about.

● Prioritize these needs and try to identify the most effective way of using the book.

for built environment professions to develop their own distinctive practices and cultures. Some see in this the dangers of inefficiency and duplication and the need for improving collaborative working.

Management is a generalist activity. Managers get things done; they achieve tasks themselves or create environments where others can work effectively. The planning, organizing, controlling and monitoring of the ways things are done, or of the processes for achieving tasks, is one of the hallmarks of management activity. Managers are like actors in the way that they act in roles which depend upon the circumstances that they face. Managers are rarely free agents with complete discretion – they tend to act as agents for others; they are constrained and even conditioned by an organization's structure, style, values and culture.

Although professionals are essentially specialists, operating within specific fields of work, they also act as managers and perform management roles. Promotion to the highest levels in an organization, however, often depends less upon the depth of specialist technical skills and more upon a breadth and balance of technical, human and conceptual skills.

The starting point for making personal development is self-knowledge. Assessing strengths and weaknesses in management terms is a positive first step towards improving management skills and qualities.

CHECKLIST OF POINTS

● What areas of technical knowledge and skill would be needed by a member of your chosen profession?
● Why might some professions develop distinctive cultures?
● Why might there be a need to improve collaborative working in the built environment?
● What activities are managers involved in?
● What are the main roles that managers perform?
● Are professionals managers?
● Why might professionals need to improve their management and business skills?

1. Lawton, A. and Rose, A. (1991) *Organization and Management in the Public Sector*, Pitman Publishing, London.
2. Muir, T. and Rance, B. (1995) *Collaborative Practices in the Built Environment*, E & FN Spon.
3. Brunsden, J. (1985) *The Nature of Management*, 2nd edn, Northwick Publishers, Worcester.
4. Wilson, C. and Rosenfeld, R.H. (1990) *Managing Organisations*, McGraw-Hill, London.
5. Koohtz, H. and Heine, W. (1990) *Essentials of Management*, McGraw-Hill, Singapore.
6. Katz, D. and Khan, R. (1978) *The Social Psychology of Organisation*, 2nd edn, Wiley, New York.
7. Pedlar, M. and Boydell, T. (1988) *Managing Yourself*, Fontana.

CHAPTER TWO

LEARNING TO LEARN

DIANA EASTCOTT AND BOB FARMER

THEME

Different people learn in different ways even when they are learning about the same thing. Managers and professionals are involved in a wide range of learning in their relationships with others and in performing and managing technical tasks. By reflecting on this learning we can become more effective and efficient in managing the process of learning. This chapter introduces ideas about learning and suggests ways of diagnosing strengths, weaknesses and blockages to learning.

OBJECTIVES

After reading this chapter you should have:

● an increase in your willingness to want to learn;

● greater ability to learn and consequently gain better marks in assessment;

● improved ability to take advantage of learning opportunities in formal situations like lectures and seminars, and informal contexts outside the 'classroom'.

This chapter will focus on the major elements in learning how to learn:

● the stages of the learning process and barriers to learning;

● individual approaches to learning and personal skills in a learning context;

● making the best use of existing learning preferences, building additional strengths and overcoming blockages in order to develop balanced learning habits;

- ways of becoming a strategic learner;

- planning to move forward and identification of a range of learning opportunities.

INTRODUCTION

As students in higher education or as professionals in the built environment, one of the most important skills you need to have in your repertoire is the skill of learning how to learn. People are often more concerned with what we learn than the specific process of how we learn. However, in order to succeed as a student and as a professional working in the built environment it is crucial to understand your own approaches to learning and how to make the most of learning opportunities. Furthermore professions in the built environment are encouraging their members to update and enhance their skills and expertise through a variety of schemes (some voluntary, some mandatory) for Continuous Professional Development (CPD). Conscious development of the skill of learning how to learn has a great many benefits.

A PROBLEM-SOLVING MODEL OF LEARNING AND BARRIERS TO LEARNING

The problem-solving model of learning on which this chapter is based is that of David Kolb.[1] The four-stage model of learning from experience which is shown in Figure 2.1 is based on the assumption that knowledge is continuously derived and tested out in the experience of the learner. Kolb's model starts from the assumption that 'ideas are not fixed and immutable elements of thought but are formed and reformed through experience'.

This model of learning from experience is a major influence in the field of learning how to learn. It is important because it acknowledges the day-to-day experience of learners, both at work and in non-educational settings, as important sources of ideas and information. These are linked by Kolb's learning cycle with information acquired through lectures, seminars, conferences, reading etc. (Figure 2.1).

The different stages in the learning cycle can be described in more detail as follows:

- **Reviewing/reflecting** – thinking through an event (e.g. a lecture or seminar) and observing the experience from many perspectives.

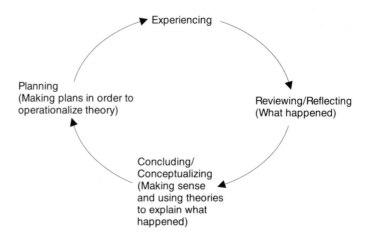

Figure 2.1   Kolb's learning cycle (adapted from Kolb[1]).

●   **Concluding/conceptualizing** – making sense of the experience and/or learning about and making sense of new ideas (theories). At university we learn many new ideas and theories.

●   **Planning** – using ideas (theories) to make decisions and to plan actions.

●   **Experiencing** – undertaking what in this context is usually a 'new' experience, e.g. undertaking a task in a different way.

The four stages must be followed in sequence but the learner can enter the cycle at any point. This cycle can also be described as a spiral (Figure 2.2) which we all go round many times learning more in different ways. Your ideas and work as a student or professional will develop and change over the years.

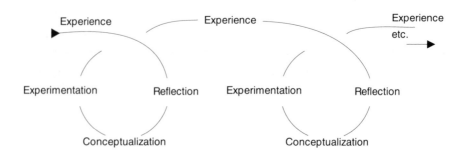

Figure 2.2   The Kolb learning cycle as a developmental spiral.

In addition to his work on the learning cycle, Kolb has made other major contributions to the study of learning how to learn. He sees all learners as different even if they are learning the same thing – in other words, individuals learn and approach problems in different ways depending on their preferred learning style. In practice this means that people vary in their interest and capacity to learn from particular stages in the learning cycle.

> Sir Nicholas Gimcrack, the archetypal mad scientist, is learning to swim by lying on a table with a thread between his teeth attached to the loins of a frog in a jam jar. Asked why he does not learn to swim in water he replies 'I seldom bring any thing to use; it's not my way.' [*The Virtuoso*, Thomas Shadwell (1676)]

Kolb suggests that, just as some people have a preference for conceptualizing and theorizing (like Sir Nicholas Gimcrack), others may prefer actions to theories.[2] Similarly on the other axis of the Kolb cycle some of you may naturally spend more of your time reflecting and observing than you would in experimenting with ideas and actively pursuing alternatives.[3] In other words there are distinct learning styles associated with each of the four stages in the learning cycle. Your own learning style will affect the way in which you react to the ideas in this book and the way in which you learn both at university and in your career in the built environment.

We will now illustrate these differences in learning style by reference to a hypothetical computing course. At the start of this course the students were set an open-ended computing problem to work on alone. After four weeks they then met to compare solutions to the problem, and also to compare the different ways in which they went about working on the problem. Three of the students displayed dramatically different styles:

● Student A went straight to a computer keyboard and started keying in segments of a programme. She did not analyse the nature of the problem. As soon as it become apparent that the programming routines being written did not work, new routines were written out and immediately tested in a trial and error way – mostly error. This student had created dozens of programming routines, none of which got close to solving the problem. She seemed not to learn from her mistakes.

- Student B appeared to start off like student A, going straight to the keyboard. He selected a procedure which he knew and implemented it. He wrote an extensive, detailed and complete programme which ran unsuccessfully but which solved a problem quite different from the one which was set. He was unaware that he had tackled the wrong problem because he was so busy getting on with the task.

- Student C became intrigued by the problem itself and its underlying features. She started reading about this kind of problem and the reading led her into related areas which also contained intriguing problems. She could talk about the topic in a general and abstract way but had not even started writing any programming code to produce a solution.

In terms of the experiential learning cycle, these students were stuck at one part of the cycle to the virtual exclusion of the other three. Each of these three students is located in Figure 2.3.

In order to learn effectively, it is necessary to utilize the abilities associated with each of the four learning styles in turn (Figure 2.4).

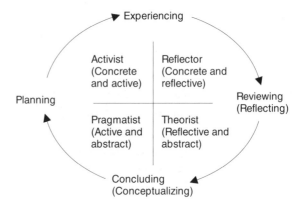

Figure 2.4 Learning styles within the Kolb cycle.

THE REFLECTION STAGE OF THE KOLB CYCLE

How do you approach learning on this course? How did you learn at school? How do you tackle the different learning tasks that you need to complete? These questions are appropriate at the reviewing or reflecting stage of the learning cycle. According to Honey and Mumford,[4] if your individual approach to learning shows a preference for reflection

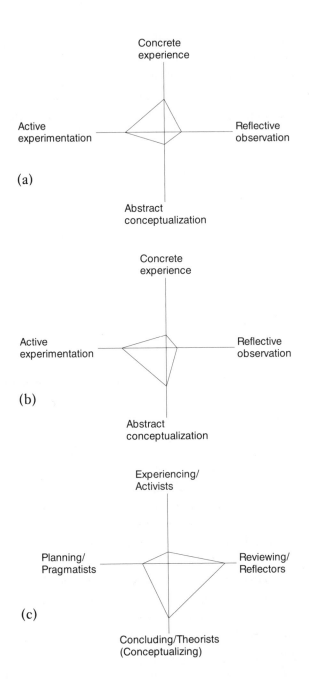

Figure 2.3 Learning profiles of (a) Student A; (b) Student B; (c) Student C.

(Figure 2.5) you will probably learn best from activities where:

● you have the opportunity to collect and analyse data, to investigate and analyse information and get to the root of a problem;
● you are asked to produce carefully considered analyses and reports;
● you can reach a decision in your own time without pressure;
● you are encouraged to stand back from events and listen/observe, e.g. observing a group at work or watching a film or video.

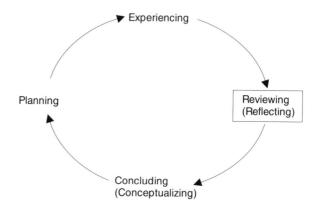

Figure 2.5   The reflection stage of the Kolb cycle: how do you approach learning?

For many people reflection in a goal-directed way is not an automatic process. Some examples of methods or activities to help with the process of reflection are given below. Please note that reflection does not have to be a solitary internal activity – it can take place in a seminar or tutorial or informally with your friends. Practising methods or activities such as these will help to strengthen your ability to reflect:

● **Learning diaries** – keep a diary of your learning. Start with a brief factual account of an event (for example, lecture, fieldwork) and go on to record your feelings and reactions.
● **Reviewing** – practice reviewing after a workshop/meeting. Try summarizing events as in Workpiece 2.1.
● **Self-assessment** – practise making self-assessments of your own work. For example, what are the strong and less strong features of an assignment or task you have recently completed? What would you like feedback on?

REVIEWING LEARNING

Things that went well

Things that could have gone better

Now try a reflection exercise for yourself (Workpiece 2.2).

REFLECTION EXERCISE

Think of a good learning experience. (It could be at school, at university, at work or a hobby or sport.) What was good about the learning experience? Jot down a few notes here:

Think of a bad learning experience. What was bad about the learning experience? Jot down a few notes here:

Now think about how you became good at one or more of the things which you listed under the category of a good learning experience.

Figure 2.6 gives some examples of responses drawn from the work of Professor Phil Race[5] when he asked the same questions of a large group of students.

In the final part of this reflection exercise think about the ways in which you are tackling the different learning tasks (Workpiece 2.3).

How do you become a conceptual learner? If your individual approach to learning is strong on concluding/conceptualizing (or, as Honey and Mumford[4] describe it, 'theorizing') (Figure 2.7), you will probably learn best from activities where:

THE CONCEPTUALIZING/ THEORIZING STAGE OF THE LEARNING CYCLE

21

Things I am good at	How I became good at it
Driving	Lessons, test, practice
Painting	Taught techniques, then practice and experimentation
Essays	Practice
Cooking	Practice, necessity, interest
Embroidery	Taught basics, practice and own mistakes
Playing clarinet	Practice, help from others, making mistakes, books, threats
Drinking beer	Extended practice, socializing
Mixing concrete	By trial and error after being shown how to do it
Table tennis	Taught, practice, time, experience, sticking with it

Figure 2.6 Examples of responses to self-assessment.[5]

WORKPIECE 2.3

LEARNING STRATEGIES

What learning strategies work well for you?

What learning strategies do not work so well for you?

- what is being considered is part of a model, system or theory;
- you have the chance to question and probe the basic methodology or logic;
- you are in structured learning situations with a clear purpose;
- you can listen to or read about ideas and concepts that emphasize rationality or logic.

The next part of the chapter concentrates on ideas which we hope will help you to improve your strategic approach to learning.

HOW TO BECOME A STRATEGIC LEARNER

More has been discovered in the past 15 years about how we learn than was known in the whole of previous history. Finding out about these discoveries can be enormously helpful to you. It will provide you with a pow-

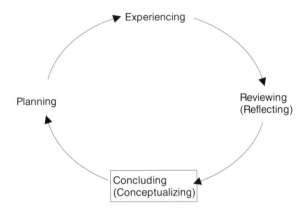

Figure 2.7 The concluding/conceptualizing stage of the Kolb cycle: how to become a conceptual learner.

erful model of what successful learners do (often quite unconsciously) and it will give you some of the tools you might choose to select and use in order to become a more motivated and effective learner.

One key piece of recent research[6] was concerned with understanding how students approached different learning tasks. This study made it clear that, for better or worse, three major influences are at work. Briefly these factors (the first two positive and the third negative) are related to the extent to which learners:

- are task oriented, and have a crystal clear idea of what it is they need to do, particularly in order to satisfy assessment requirements;
- are looking for meaning in their studies by interacting in an positive way with what is being learnt;
- rely almost completely on rote learning and approach learning tasks with the intention of reproducing what it is that they are studying.

These factors profoundly affect the quality of our learning. However, careful consideration will confirm your suspicions that successful learning is as much to do with the way that courses are taught and assessed as it is with the way that students approach learning tasks. We can all recall courses which gave us very little time and opportunity for deep understanding and which rewarded our ability to reproduce large chunks of factual material. (Remember A-levels?)

As a learner, what can you do to help yourself? We will look at a number of possibilities under three headings:

- becoming more task oriented;
- looking for meaning;
- using reflection and review to improve your memory.

Before we begin, however, we should emphasize that these are very much options and that it is up to you to pick and choose the techniques that appeal to you and which suit the context in which you are learning. We have already seen that people's learning styles differ greatly. It is unlikely that any individual will adopt all of these strategies.

BECOMING MORE TASK ORIENTED

Workpiece 2.4 offers some suggestions to help you to think more about strategic approaches to studying.

LOOKING FOR MEANING

When we learn about something in a 'deep way' we use, often unconsciously, strategies which help us to look for meaning in what we are studying.

For example, if you are reading a difficult journal article or solving a problem or designing something and you become really interested in what you are doing, you will often quite naturally take a 'deep' approach. On the other hand, if you take a 'surface' approach to learning, your intention (again often unconsciously) is probably to 'remember' the wretched material, or simply get the 'right' answers or have done with the task as soon as possible. You'll be pleased to know that taking surface approaches is nothing to do with a lack of intelligence. In fact if your tutors have given you too much to do and too little time in which to do it, the smart approach might be to say, 'Okay, I'll just learn it.' You would then probably rely on your skills at cleverly reproducing whatever it was that your tutor wanted.

Surface approaches are very common; we have all worked in this manner at some time or another. However, you should be aware that, apart from being tedious and terribly boring, this way of studying is often associated with high drop-out rates and with failure.

Knowledge of the concept of 'deep' and 'surface' approaches is an important factor in understanding the process of 'learning how to learn'.

Workpiece 2.5 shows some techniques that will help you to look for meaning in what you are studying. (This is a creative activity which will appeal to learners with highly visual learning styles.)

STRATEGIES FOR STUDYING

Options	Your checklist (tick)	
	I do this already	Worth a try

1. Create a positive view of where you are going with your studying.
   - How will gaining your qualification affect your life in the future? Think success!
   - Draw a map giving an overview of the content of your course (see Mind Maps in Workpiece 2.6, Figure 2.9 and Chapter 3).
2. Find out about assessment requirements.
   - Get to know what your tutors really require of you.
   - Look at past examination papers.
   - Talk to students who have completed the course/module and find out what is important.
   - Find out what makes for a good essay/project/assignment.
3. Plan your time.
   - Set yourself realistic goals.
   - Make 'to do' lists.
   - Keep a diary or a wall planner.
   - Break down 'elephant tasks' such as projects into manageable chunks.
   - Start with the 'worst' bit first.
   - Plan your study time and break it up with 5-minute mini-breaks.
   - Give yourself little rewards when you have finished something.

USING REFLECTION AND REVIEW TO IMPROVE YOUR MEMORY

As authors of this chapter, it would have been tempting for us to refer to some library books about study skills and to reproduce in this section a whole range of tricks for helping you to improve your memory. However, apart from it being a classic example of 'surface approach' to learning, this would constitute bad advice since what we are aiming to do is to introduce you to the concept of learning how to learn.

Memory is obviously very important to us and the best way to remember something is to understand it. (Think how difficult it would be to remember a long series of nonsense words.) How can we use 'deep

WORKPIECE 2.5

LOOKING FOR MEANING

Options	Your checklist (tick)	
	I do this already	Worth a try

When you are reading a book or completing an assignment, ask yourself difficult, fundamental 'key' questions about what you are doing. For example:

- Reason – giving questions like 'Why?'
- Central – questions like 'What?'
- Explaining – questions like 'How?'

Put your thoughts into words. For example:

- Discuss 'new' material with a friend.
- Encourage questions; write down answers in your own words/pictures.
- Ask each other how you solved a problem. (Working with a 'study-buddy' in this conscious way is a very powerful technique for taking deep approaches.)

Make comparisons. For example, how is 'X' different from and the same as 'Y' (something you are already familiar with)?

Represent 'new' ideas in as many ways as possible. For example, words, pictures, flow diagrams, algorithms, graphs, analogies.

approaches' and better understanding to improve our recall of important concepts and principles? The very obvious answer to this is 'plenty of revision'. This may sound tedious, but Workpiece 2.6 (and Figure 2.8) suggests some options for helping you to reflect and review.

The option of **creating summaries** – for example, a half-page summary of important lectures – should appeal to learners with a more verbal learning style.

Mind mapping[7] is a technique (Figure 2.9) which enables you to summarize and display ideas in a way that is economical, creative and highly visual:

- to summarize;
- to plan;

REVISION AND REFLECTION TO IMPROVE MEANING

Options	Your checklist (tick)	
	I do this already	Worth a try

Use planned time intervals for review. This technique calls for effective goal setting skills and good time management. The gain in recall from employing a programme of 'quick reviews' can be considerable (Figure 2.8).

Use 'down time', for example do a quick bit of mind mapping and reviewing when you are sitting on the bus.

Summarize your notes from conferences/lectures. Do this in your own words, no more than one page of A4. Do it immediately.

Make the activity a creative exercise by using mind maps.

Use revision to improve understanding.

Time spent questioning and refining your summaries is more effective than time spent testing for recall.

The more you understand the more you remember.

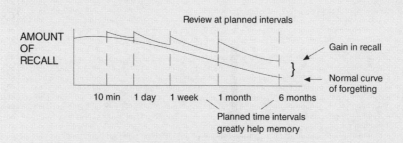

Figure 2.8   Using planned time intervals to assist recall.

- to recall;
- to review.

In this final planning stage (Figure 2.10) we invite you to look at the checklists in Workpieces 2.4, 2.5 and 2.6 and to note those items that you have identified as 'worth having a try'. These can now become the

THE PLANNING STAGE OF THE KOLB CYCLE

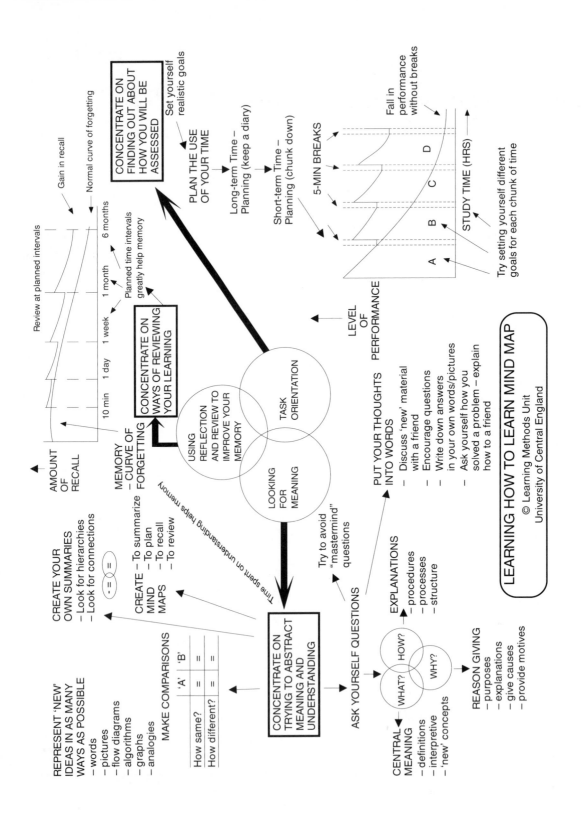

Figure 2.9 Example of a mind map: learning how to learn

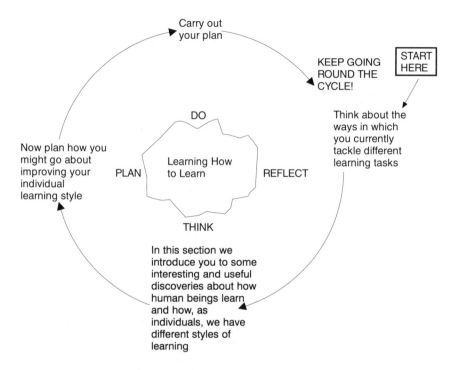

Figure 2.10 The planning stage of the Kolb cycle: planning how to move forward. The four stages in the cycle are summarized.

basis of your action plan. An action plan is simply a written list of things to do.

It is essential to see yourself now as being being involved in a series of small experiments in which you are in control of the experimental design. Our final piece of advice would be to suggest that you take an incremental approach and that you are more likely to succeed if you share your triumphs and traumas with a friend who is also determined to take an active role in learning how to learn.

By reflecting on how they learn, professionals and managers can become more effective in managing the process of learning and the changes involved. This conscious development of the skill of 'learning how to learn' has the benefit of increasing both the desire and the ability to learn. In particular it enhances the ability to identify and take advantage of opportunities for learning. This skill is particularly useful for professionals who have a need, throughout their careers, to identify ways of updating and enhancing their professional skills and expertise and meeting the requirements of professional bodies for undertaking programmes of Continuous Professional Development (CPD).

SUMMARY

David Kolb's 'learning cycle' of doing, reflecting, theorizing and planning has been a major influence in the field of learning how to learn. It starts from the assumption that 'ideas are not fixed and immutable elements of thought' but 'are formed and reformed through experience'. This model acknowledges that the day-to-day learning experiences of learners at work, in non-educational settings, are important sources of learning and information.

Each of the four stages of the learning cycle is associated with distinct learning styles. Each of us learns and approaches problems in different ways, depending on our preference for one or other of these styles. As specific abilities have been identified with each learning style it is possible to develop them and therefore to improve the overall balance of our learning habits. For a student to achieve this balance and become a 'strategic learner' there are a number of possible approaches, including: becoming more task orientated; looking for meaning; and using reflection and review to improve memory.

Your own learning style will affect the way in which you react to the ideas in this book and the way in which you learn at university and throughout your career in the built environment.

CHECKLIST OF POINTS

- Why is 'learning to learn' important for professionals and managers?
- What are the four stages of Kolb's learning cycle?
- What learning styles are associated with each stage in the 'learning cycle'?
- What abilities are associated with each of the learning styles?
- How can you become more task oriented?
- What techniques could you use to help you 'look for meaning'?
- What is your action plan for becoming a 'strategic learner'?

REFERENCES

1. Kolb, D.A. (1984) *Experiential learning – experience as the source of learning and development*, Prentice Hall, New Jersey.
2. Kolb, D.A., Rubin, L. and McIntyre, J. (1984) *Organisational psychology: an experiential approach*, Prentice Hall, New Jersey.
3. Eastcott, D. and Farmer, R. (1992) *Planning teaching for active learning. Effective Learning and Teaching in Higher Education, Module 3*, CVCP Universities Staff Development and Training Unit.
4. Honey, P. and Mumford, A. (1986) *The manual of learning styles*, Peter Honey, Berkshire.

5. Race, P. (1993) *Never mind the teaching, feel the learning*, SEDA Paper 80, Staff and Educational Development Association.

6. Entwistle, N.J. and Ramsden, P. (1983) *Understanding student learning*, Croom Helm, London.

7. Russell, P. (1979) *The Brain Book*, Routledge and Kegan Paul, London.

PERSONAL AND SELF-MANAGEMENT SKILLS

ANNE HILL

THEME

Everyone has a level of personal and self-management skills derived from both their educational and their life experiences. In the built environment we need to develop or enhance skills to work more effectively; to give presentations to a range of people and organizations; and to manage our time well in order to cope with the stress of increased workloads and the pressure to perform.

This chapter examines ways we can build on those skills to help us to become more effective in the way we work.

OBJECTIVES

After reading this chapter you should be able to:

● study effectively by reading what you need to read, writing to meet a brief and producing work to deadlines;

● give an effective verbal presentation in a range of situations;

● use the computer technology appropriate to your field of work;

● manage your time by analysing what you do now, planning for your future and using techniques to organize the time available.

INTRODUCTION

Why consider the skills discussed in this chapter? Built environment students and practitioners work in demanding, challenging and competitive environments. We need to manage ourselves, our time and our resources if we are to succeed. The sections in this chapter offer practical ideas and techniques that can be practised and used to great effect. In a number of places there are practical exercises for you to try. (Use the Kolb learning circle mentioned in Chapter 2 to try out ideas, consider what happened and what you learned and to plan for the next time.)

Why are personal skills useful to students and practitioners in the built environment? You already need to read an enormous amount of material to keep yourself up to date with new developments, techniques, legal issues and what potentially your competitors are doing. You need to sort your material into logical order. You need to be able to write reports to present factual written information to clients, managers, staff and committees. A well-written report is a most effective way to get information to others because reports are arranged in a way which makes it easy for anyone to read the information that matters to them quickly, without having to search for the interesting point.

Let us now examine each element of these skills.

READING SKILLS

When did you learn to read? When you were at infant school? At home with your parents and family? How did you learn to read? We learn word by word, line by line, from first page to last. This is fine for reading a detective, romance or sci-fi novel but it is not necessarily appropriate for research or investigation. When you find yourself with a long reading list for each topic you are studying, or a topic to research with a wealth of written information to sort through, or a pile of technical journals you want to read but which must be passed on to others, the thought of reading everything may be quite daunting. Here is the good news: you don't have to read everything. It is far better to be selective in your reading and to choose what you need to read in detail.

WORKPIECE 3.1

READING SKILLS

Time yourself reading the section on planning and organizing material in the presentation skills section of this chapter.

How long did you take?
If it took you more than 2 minutes you could improve your reading speed.

So how do you read more quickly?

SCAN THE MATERIAL FIRST

- Use the list of chapters to give you clues to the information you need.
- Use the index at the back of the book to find key points and where they are in the book.
- In a magazine, scan the index or review the article headings.
- Use the summary or conclusions to see if a report covers material you want.
- Check the first sentence of each paragraph. This should tell you what is going to be covered in the following sentences.

PRACTISE SPEED READING

- Our brains take in information much more quickly than we can talk. Don't read aloud. Moving your lips means you must use every word.
- Find key words rather than reading every word one by one.
- Read more than one word at a time.
- Practise reading two words in the sentence together, then take in three or four words at a time.
- Move your eyes down the centre of the page, rather than from left to right across the line. Use your finger to guide your eyes down the centre at first. Later you should not need to guide your eyes.
- You should find you are able to read more quickly using these techniques, but they do require you to practise this reading skill.

WORKPIECE 3.2

SPEED READING

Without referring back to the section on presentation skills you read earlier, can you answer the following questions?

- How many points are there in the checklist? Can you list them?

- What is signposting?
- What is more important than being word perfect?

Check your answers against the text.
How did you do? Could you remember all the points?

MAKE BRIEF NOTES

- We don't need to rely on memory to make sense of and recall material. Don't start to read without a pen and paper at your side.

Make notes of key points which will remind you of what you read and where you read it so you can easily return to the same text.

● If the text belongs to you, you could also use a highlighter pen or a pencil to mark key words. But never, never make notes in a library book or one loaned by someone else!

● You then need to sort out what you read and when you read it. It isn't always possible to find the time to read everything at the time you find the information. You could be working on a different assignment, or be about to go into a meeting or a lecture.

● Every time you see something you think might be useful make a note of where and when. For example, if you are glancing at a periodical and see something that might be useful later make a note of the date and edition number, the page number and title of the article. Keep your notes in one place; for example, slip such notes into a special file.

WORKPIECE 3.3

MAKING NOTES

Practise making notes of your sources.
Use a file to store them for future reference.

These techniques will save you valuable time and make research for your writing or your reading for information much easier and more effective.

CHECKLIST
● Be selective in your reading.
● Scan material first.
● Practise speed reading techniques.
● Make notes of your reading.
● Make notes of your sources.

We have already discussed the need to make notes and to record useful information found when reading. In order to sort your reading and research into a logical order you could use a list or a mind map.

ORGANIZING YOUR MATERIAL

● Write down what you have to do first. Underline any key words that give you clues about what you need to do and how you need to do it.

LISTS

● Write down in a list everything you need to include in the assignment or task you have to complete. Then use numbers or letters to sort the list into a logical order, point 1 or (a) for the first thing to be done or written, point 2 or (b) for the next, and so on.

MIND MAPS

Some people find mind maps useful as an alternative to lists. Use a blank sheet of paper and in the centre write down your task and circle it. As ideas come to you write down what you need to do or to include around the title in the centre. Link connecting ideas by lines. Then number or letter the topics in the order they need to be completed or written (as for the list).

Figure 2.9 (Chapter 2) gave an example of a mind map.

WORKPIECE 3.4

MIND MAPPING

Write out a list or draw a mind map of how you get ready for the day. It could include how you prepare in the bathroom (shower or bath, shave or make up or hair, cleaning teeth, etc.), get breakfast (if you do) or travel to college or work.

Next, try using this technique for your next assignment or work task.

CHECKLIST
● Write down your task.
● Find the key words or clues about what you need to do.
● Write a list or draw a mind map.
● Arrange your points or actions in order.

WRITING SKILLS

You will be asked to write essays at college or university, but at work you are more likely to be asked to write reports. Let us look at both essay and report writing in more detail.

ESSAYS

An essay is a continuous piece of writing, set out in paragraphs. It is usually a response to a question or a title given by a tutor. An essay is a way of demonstrating your understanding of a topic.

You do this in writing, by clearly indicating what you have found through research and by explaining how you have reached your opinions on a subject by informed comment. Comment must be based on the logical interpretation of the work of others or of your own research.

Essays should have a clear introduction, a main body and a conclusion. Figure 3.1 and Workpiece 3.5 explain what you should do when writing an essay.

You should:	Skills	Place in the essay
Demonstrate you have understood the question or title you have been given, or have set for yourself.	Skills demonstrated will include analysis and demonstrate that you have been able to distinguish between all the elements of the question.	This should happen in the introduction.
Have researched and collected all the relevant material.	Skills demonstrated will include your ability to research material from a wide variety of sources. Use your speed reading techniques here.	Before you start to write. You could use a list or mind map to help to arrange material in a logical order.
Have planned how you will write the essay so the reader can follow your reasoning logically.	Planning, logical thinking, good preparation.	Write a rough plan before you write the essay. It ensures you do not leave out any key points. You can check that everything to answer the question is there before you start to write.
Have organized material in a logical order.	Your organization, a clear structure.	The main body of the essay.
Be able to write your answer in a clear, comprehensive and cohesive (easily followed) way.	How you write and communicate including good use of grammar, punctuation and paragraphs. Logical order.	Throughout your essay.
Have demonstrated your ability to analyse and evaluate material and make it clear how what you have written relates to the question or title of the essay.	Critical thought, your presentation of arguments, weighing and making judgements about your research.	Main body and conclusions.

Figure 3.1 Writing essays.

WORKPIECE 3.5

PLANNING YOUR ESSAY

When you next have an essay to write, make a plan of action before you start.

- Look for the key words in the question.
- What are you being asked to do?

- When is it to be ready – how long have you got to research and plan it?

Devise your plan based on your available time and use a list or mind map to arrange everything in logical order.

We will now examine the structure of the essay.

THE INTRODUCTION   The introduction sets out your plan of writing for the essay. In the introduction you tell the reader what they are going to find in the rest of the essay, in the order in which you plan to present your arguments. The introduction should be no more than two or three paragraphs.

Tell them what you are going to tell them.

THE MAIN BODY   The main body presents the detail of your discussions, your research and your arguments. It is the 'meat' (or cheese, if you are vegetarian) of the essay.

Tell them.

THE CONCLUSION   The conclusion is where you sum up your findings and from the evidence reach your own conclusions about the subject of the question or title. You must never introduce new material in your conclusions.

Tell them what you have told them – together with conclusions from the evidence you have presented.

REFERENCES   You must source your material. If you have used information from any source you should make a note of where you found it, both in the text and in the reference section. The only time you can 'get away' with not having a full reference list is in an examination, when you may not be able to recall sources accurately. You should still credit your sources in the text.

If you do not reference your writing you may be accused of plagiarism (taking and using someone else's thoughts or words as if they are your own). Plagiarism is considered very serious and any written work submitted at college and not referenced may not be accepted or marked as a 'fail'.

Check with your own college for their preferred method of referencing.

There are some basic rules. Include: the author's name; the year of publication; the title of the book (or article in a periodical); the volume or exact date if it is a periodical; the publisher and, if it is published outside the UK, the country of publication. In the text put the author's name and date, in brackets, after the relevant text.

No more than 10% of your work should be direct quotes from other sources.

WORKPIECE 3.6

REFERENCING

Look in both this and three other text books and see how references are organized. Practise making notes of all your sources.

When you have written your essay you must check it for the following:

- Have I answered the question?
- Have I covered the main points I wanted to include?
- Are the spelling and grammar right? If you are using a word processor you may be able to use a 'spellcheck'. Some programs do include grammar checks, but these are often tailored for American rather than British grammar.

CHECKLIST
- Examine the question or title for key words.
- Do your research.
- Plan your essay carefully – use a list or mind map to arrange in a logical order.
- Will your plan ensure that you answer the question?
- Ensure that you have an introduction, a main body and a conclusion.
- Check that you have no new points in the conclusion.
- Check that you have referenced all your sources.
- Check your work for spelling and grammar.
- Keep one copy for yourself.

REPORT WRITING

Reports are written to inform, consult, analyse and evaluate material. They are structured in such a way that they are easy for the reader to find the topic or area which interests them without always having to read the whole document. Reports are used in all the built environment professions. Architects and others prepare briefs in a report format; planners, quantity surveyors, housing professionals and others use reports to inform committees and individuals so that decisions can be made, weighing all the relevant information.

Reports have a clear structure and they may have up to nine distinct and separate parts. The longer or more formal the report, the more elements will need to be used.

As with essays, you must carry out thorough research, arrange material in a logical order and write clearly. You should summarize your findings and either reach conclusions or make recommendations.

Figure 3.2 examines the nine elements of a report.

Element	Purpose	When to use
1. Title page	A brief title, possibly with a more detailed explanation, the author's name, date and who requested the report or its purpose.	In a formal report. In a less formal report you would have your heading, name and purpose at the top of the first page of the report.
2. Contents list	To direct the reader through the report to any part that they wish to read.	Usually in a long report. Pages must be numbered and each section or chapter should also be numbered (1, 2, 2.1) or lettered (A, B, a, b, etc.). Keep numbering consistent.
3. Abstract	No more than 80–100 words, it is the report in miniature. It must be capable of standing alone as it is separate from the main report. Used by libraries so researchers can look through abstracts and see if the full report will include material or findings they wish to read.	In a formal report. Theses usually have abstracts.
4. Introduction	The introduction explains what, why, when, where and how. It covers who asked for the report, its purpose, the terms of reference and limitations, the background and your method of working and sources of material.	In all reports there should be a clear introduction.
5. Discussion	The main body of the report, arranged in a logical order, using separate sections for each topic area. Organize material using the following: ● The most important information first. ● Next most important. ● Next most important, etc. A report is not a detective novel, with the key to the puzzle on the last page.	In any report.

Figure 3.2 Writing reports.

PLANNING YOUR REPORT

Plan a short report based on the list or mind map you devised for Workpiece 3.4. Choose headings and subheadings. Number (or letter) the report plan.

CHECKLIST

- Define the purpose of the report (using one sentence).
- Do your research.
- Plan your work using a list or mind map.
- Write your discussion first, then summary and recommendations, then introduction.
- Write your contents list last.
- Check that your appendices and references are all in place.
- Check for spelling and grammar.
- Check how many copies are required and supply them – keep a copy for yourself.

PRESENTATION SKILLS

All professionals in the built environment are required to make presentations at some point in their career. Students are asked to present their learning through presentations to lecturers. Potential interviewees are increasingly asked to make presentations as an integral part of the job interview. Employees are asked to make presentations to committees and boards of management, to clients and to groups such as tenants, councillors or the general public. Managers are required to make presentations to many of the same groups and to present information to staff and to trainees. Self-employed people have to convince potential clients and one very effective way to do this is to use a presentation.

Presentations can be daunting, standing up in front of others and being on show. Typical fears are: being boring; 'drying up' in front of the audience; the audience asking questions to which you do not know the answers; showing how nervous you are and making a fool of yourself.

If your presentation is well prepared and you follow some simple guidelines, presentations remain an effective way of delivering information to groups and to other individuals. This section considers how to deliver an effective presentation.

PLANNING AND ORGANIZING MATERIAL

WHAT ARE YOUR OBJECTIVES?   Your first task is to check what the focus of your topic is to be. You need to be clear about the degree of detail or how technical the presentation must be, or know the 'rules' that will apply. You also need to check who is your likely audience and what they expect from the presentation.

DO YOUR RESEARCH   Read reports or books or speak to other practitioners to ensure that you are up to date. Use post-its, lists or mind maps to order your material.

SIGNPOST THE PRESENTATION   Plan to take your audience with you by telling them where they are, where they are going and, when they have been there, where they have been. Does the presentation follow a logical order? Do your items go in a straight line from A to B or do you meander off at tangents? Avoid branches, but you can have loops that bring you back to where you can move on.

WRITE A SCRIPT   Like an actor you will learn the final version. Put it to one side for one or two days. Then read and review it. Edit your material. Read it through aloud. How long did it take? Too much material? Not enough? Did it make sense? Was it appropriate?

Rewrite your script and now learn it. You should never read from a prepared script. It is boring for the audience and makes you look as if you don't know your subject well. Use small prompt cards with key words or phrases. It is even better to rely on your visual aids. If they are in the right and logical order these are much better than cards. However, cards are better than A4 sheets of paper. Remember, it is not being word perfect that counts but a good, warm, confident voice delivering well-organized material.

PLAN   Plan your visual aids and any work you want the audience to do, including any question session at the end. Visual aids include prepared flipchart sheets, blank flipchart sheets if you are asking the audience to give you ideas, overhead slides, 35-mm slides, videos, plans and models, equipment or materials for the audience to handle. The list isn't exhaustive but these are the most common. Be wary of using too many: they can confuse and make the presentation seem disjointed.

PRACTISE THE COMPLETE PRESENTATION   Practise with a friend or colleague. Ask them to time you and comment honestly about your manner, voice and material. Review what you have achieved.

PRESENTATION – YOUR KEY POINTS

You are asked to present some information about an activity that interests you.
List the key points and how you might get your message across so that others will also be interested.

Did any of the following appear on your list in Workpiece 3.8?

EXERCISE

- Introduction – who you are, what you are going to talk about and why.
- Main part – what you are talking about in detail. Visual aids demonstration?
- What order you should use, e.g. how you started, what you do now, what you get out of it, should others try it and how would they get started?
- Audience participation – listening, activity, questions during or after?
- Enthusiasm – fun, serious? Layout of room to help you?
- Body language – tone of voice, smile, standing, sitting?
- How to let the audience know when the topic changes or ends?
- Conclusions.

CHECKLIST
- Do your research.
- Plan your material.
- Signpost your material.
- Sort your material.
- Plan your visual aids.
- Rehearse.

Be aware of what you are saying and how you are saying it. Be enthusiastic about your topic, even if you think it is dry. Enthusiasm is infectious. Smile at the audience, at least when you first face them. This shows them you value them and welcome their attention. If your message is serious, look grave but not angry. Stay calm.
    Deliver your presentation in the following way:

**DELIVERING A
PRESENTATION**

● Introduction – tell them who you are, why you are the speaker and what you are going to tell them.

● Main ideas and points – tell them. If you are trying to persuade, use benefits as well as features.

● Summary – tell them what you have told them.

POSTURE   Keep yourself erect but not stiff. Stand up with your feet slightly apart and pointing towards the audience and your weight evenly distributed. Avoid leaning on one hip, then the other. The shifting can be distracting for the audience.

STAND RATHER THAN SIT   You have more control and the audience can all see you. One of the easiest ways to lose an audience is to disappear from their sight. If you wish to sit to take questions, perch on the front of a table or on a chair back. If you wish to stand behind a table or at a lectern, this is permissible, but consider the message you are sending to your audience. Are you hiding, avoiding them or trying to intimidate them (teacher syndrome)? If you stand at a lectern, don't clutch the sides for support and show 'white knuckles' to your audience.

MOVEMENT   Although you want to avoid pacing around, you also want to avoid playing 'statues'. Both distract the audience. Some movement – a pace forward or to the side, coming out from behind a table, standing to the side of the lectern – are all interesting.

GESTURES   Be natural. Purists say that it is distracting if you wave your hands about but it can also convey passion or enthusiasm. Open gestures can include your audience and keep their attention.

There are some ways of keeping you hands under control that look worse than using your hands naturally. These include having your hands in your pockets and fiddling with keys or change, keeping your hands behind your back or on your hips or folding your arms, which makes you look defensive.

EYE CONTACT   Maintain eye contact with your audience. This does mean looking at the individuals in the audience, but not catching someone's eye for more than 1–3 seconds. If your audience is large you can look slightly over their heads, ensuring that you look at all sides of the room. However, remember you are not at Wimbledon. If you look rapidly from side to side you will get dizzy and so will your audience.

FEEDBACK ON YOUR PREPARATION

Design a checklist of what you would like honest feedback on. It could be how you organized the material, how you appear when delivering material, for example voice, gestures, mannerisms you need to be aware of (I wear glasses and constantly push them back up my nose – even when they have not slipped!), how you handled visual aids, how the audience felt after watching the presentation.

CHECKLIST

- Be enthusiastic.
- Consider delivery:
  - tell them what you are going to tell them;
  - tell them;
  - tell them what you have told them.
- Consider your posture, movement and gestures.
- Maintain eye contact with your audience.

USING VISUAL AIDS

People are more likely to remember your message or to understand what you are aiming for if they have something to look at whilst they listen to your presentation. It helps you to keep your presentation in order and to offer your audience 'signposts' to where they are and where they are going. There are various visual aids that can be used and some golden rules for using them.

- Plan what visual aids you will use – what is available, what is suitable for the size of the audience and the size of the room. Do not use too many different types of visual aid in one presentation; it can overwhelm the audience and there is also more to go wrong.
- Rehearse using the visual aids – practise using the equipment, check sightlines for the audience, know what to do if the equipment goes wrong and have a contingency plan if it does. Do not wait until the presentation is about to start before finding out that the equipment is not there or is not working.

CHECKLIST

- Plan what visual aids you will use.
- Do not use too many at one time.

- Check your equipment before the presentation.
- Have contingency plans if the equipment goes wrong.
- Practise using the visual aids.

Let us examine the most commonly used and most easily accessible visual aids with some hints on how to use them.

OVERHEAD PROJECTOR AND SLIDES   Often people are quite nervous of using this most common and useful piece of equipment. The overhead projector can be used to disastrous effect, but if you follow some simple rules it can work very effectively.

DESCRIPTION   The OHP (as it is usually called) reflects light on to or through an acetate sheet and then on to a screen, using a pair of mirrors. Acetates can be printed, photocopied or hand written, although each method of producing information requires a different type of acetate sheet. Special pens are used to handwrite or draw on an acetate. For photocopies you must use a heat-resistant acetate or you will find that it has melted into the photocopier and you will be extremely unpopular!

HOW TO USE THE OHP   Do not put too much information on each acetate. Avoid merely copying typewritten text on to an acetate as it isn't easy to read. Use a large typeface or font (at least 16–18 points, in bold). Acetates are put onto the OHP the right way up so that you, as the presenter, can read the material easily.

Switch the OHP off between acetates and position your next one before switching back on. Check the position of the reflection on the screen every time you switch the OHP on. It is surprising how few people do this and the audience find themselves trying to read off the ceiling. Focusing is normally by moving the mirrors up and down on their column. The further away the OHP is from the screen, the larger the reflection on the screen. However, go too far and you will have trouble focusing.

Check that the equipment works before you start your presentation. If it isn't working, find out who to ask for help. If the light bulb goes out, there is usually a spare bulb in the machine. You should be able to change the bulb easily, using the small lever (and explanatory diagram) on the front of the modern OHP.

Check the audience's sightlines. Can they see the screen? Where will you stand so that you don't block anyone's view?

Be careful about reading directly from the screen – you could find yourself talking to the wall instead of to your audience. Stand to the side and glance back and forth between screen and audience. Alternatively, use a pen to point to the part of the acetate you want to highlight – on the acetate, not the screen.

You could use a piece of paper, covering the acetate and revealing your information piece by piece. The paper will blank out the light and prevent the audience from being distracted by other information too early. Practise and find the technique that suits you best.

WHEN TO USE THE OHP For presentations to groups of up to approximately 150 people. If the gathering is much larger than this the OHP acetates may be indistinct.

FLIPCHARTS Flipcharts can be prepared in advance or used for instant information during the presentation.

DESCRIPTION Flipcharts are A1 sized sheets of paper, with a stand or some other method of hanging them at eye level.

HOW TO USE FLIPCHARTS Using broad, coloured felt pens and big, bold print for instant information, it doesn't matter if it is neat, or spelt correctly. It does matter that it is neat and spelt correctly if it is prepared in advance.

WHEN TO USE FLIPCHARTS Flipcharts are best used for instant information; for example, brainstorming ideas coming from the audience, or for developing ideas. They are not suitable for groups of more than 20–30 as they will not be visible from too far away. Flipchart sheets can be taken away after the presentation and the ideas developed if you wish.

CHALKBOARDS These are still common in universities and colleges. You need chalk and a board rubber or cloth. Be careful not to wipe the chalkdust on to your clothes. Use in the same way as flipcharts, but you can't take the ideas away with you.

WHITEBOARDS Whiteboards are similar to chalkboards and flipcharts, but you must use special whiteboard pens or your work will not rub off when you finish.

35-MM SLIDES AND PROJECTORS These are one of the most expensive visual aids but they look very professional. You can project photographs or, increasingly, text that audiences can see easily. Projectors can have carousels for up to 100 slides, or cartridges holding up to 30 slides.

HOW TO USE 35-MM SLIDES   Using slides involves preparation well before the presentation. Check the equipment before you start any presentation as slides might be loaded upside down. The projector is usually mounted on a special stand so that it projects a large enough image on the screen. You need to be able to black out the room, which means that you are likely to be talking to your audience in the dark. You must be very confident of your material as you will not be able to rely upon notes.

WHEN TO USE 35-MM SLIDES   The slides can be used to show and describe photographs (for example, building sites, designs, equipment) and also to present notes visible to large groups, where the OHP would not be so clear.

VIDEOS OR 16-MM FILM   These media are expensive to produce but very professional looking if used correctly. They are suitable for pre-prepared or off-the-shelf material.

HOW TO USE VIDEOS OR FILMS   Use them to illustrate points, but is it your own work? You need the correct projection equipment; for example, television and video playback machine or 16-mm projector and screen. It is now quite unusual to use 16-mm films but some archive material is still not available on video. You must check that the equipment is available (it often needs to be booked in advance). You need to check sound levels, and set the tape or film ready to go when you need it.

WHEN TO USE VIDEOS OR FILMS   Videos are useful for illustrating points and showing pre-recorded interviews; 16-mm projectors for showing archive material. Unless you have large screen facilities, videos are not effective with groups of more than 30–40 as people cannot see the television screen.

MODELS, PLANS, DRAWINGS, EQUIPMENT   These items might be appropriate for showing smaller groups your ideas or demonstrating use. Groups must be able to gather around the model, plan table or drawing and see what you are talking about. They may need to handle equipment. Again, using these visual aids requires forward planning. You can't leave it until the last minute.

Presentations can be given singly or in groups. It is relatively easy when you are on your own as you rely only on your own resources and you are responsible for what happens. Presenting in teams is different and can look very polished or very poor.

RESPONSIBILITY   If you are asked to make a team presentation you need to decide who takes responsibility for which element of the presentation. However, you should always remember that everyone remains responsible for ensuring that tasks are completed on time, material is researched and prepared and equipment is organized and working.

KNOWLEDGE   Every member of the team must be familiar with the whole of the presentation. A common pitfall is to learn your own material and not know what others have done. The risks of repetition, omissions or a lack of coordination are the end results of everyone doing their own thing and thinking it will work on the day.

COORDINATION   Plan your material so that as far as possible there is continuity, style and professionalism about the whole. This doesn't mean that individuals must lose their particular identity or strengths. Ideas for a coordinated feel include clear introductions, the same style or approach to visual aids (perhaps one person could prepare them all) and the same amount of time for each person, with careful clock-watching so that one person doesn't overrun. If you are not presenting you must remember you are still on show as part of the team. Keep still and calm. Don't start gossiping with your neighbour. Be alert so that you can help if something goes wrong for your team mates.

SIGNPOSTS   It becomes even more important to let the audience know what is happening throughout the presentation. There are more messages to get confused in a team presentation. Greet the audience; introduce each person and their role at the beginning; hand over, using names, to the person following on; tell the audience what is happening in each section; tell the audience where they have been; summarize the whole presentation and ensure that they are clear when it is over. You could decide to use a 'compere' to bring individuals on and off centre stage. Thank each other as you hand over or take over. Use appropriate visual aids to keep the audience interested.

PRACTISE THE PRESENTATION   Rehearse using visual aids, checking your timings and material. Check your venue and set it up to suit you and the team. Keep the team together, perhaps to one side, so that there are no delays in handover from one person to the next. Review the presentation and ensure that no key elements are missing and it is in a logical order.

CONTINGENCY PLANNING   Particularly if a team member is late or ill, can you adapt the material to cover the gap? Ensure that everyone is familiar with the material and that your own material is available for others to use in case you cannot be there.

CHECKLIST
- Everyone is responsible for the presentation.
- Everyone knows the whole presentation.
- Coordination.
- Signpost and let the audience know what is happening.
- Practise together.
- Make contingency plans.

COPING TECHNIQUES

COPING WITH QUESTIONS   Often when you make a presentation you will be asked questions by the audience, either during or after the session. Your response can be based upon the type of question and by 'reading' the hidden message sent by the questioner.

THE GENUINE ENQUIRY   The questioner wants some information. They may not have understood something you have said and wish to clarify a point or take the discussion further. This is reasonable and most questions you are asked will be of this type.

Answer honestly. If you need time to think of a reply, either nod to show that you have heard and are attending to the question, think quietly for a few seconds or use stalling phrases to give yourself a little time to think.

EXAMPLE:
'That is an interesting question . . . I would like to take a moment to consider it.'

You only need a moment to reflect. Alternatively ask the speaker to repeat the question. This also gives you time to put your thoughts in order, particularly if you do not understand the question as phrased.

If you cannot answer the question, be honest and say you do not know – but could find out and get back to the speaker. If you think this is too embarrassing, another tactic is to ask the speaker to come and discuss the question with you after the session.

EXAMPLE:
'That is an interesting point. I am not able to discuss it at the moment but if you see me later . . .'

Repeat the question, addressing it to the whole audience. Someone will respond if you wait long enough. It may even be the person who asked the question.

EXAMPLE:
'Jo has just asked xxxx. What do you think?'

ULTERIOR MOTIVES However, some audiences have other motives. Who is the person with an ulterior motive to catch you out? This individual usually wants to show off their own 'superior' knowledge. Let them. Respond using phrases like 'That's very interesting. What do you think?', directed at the questioner only. If the answer provides you with new information, thank them. They usually preen!

If what they say is rubbish or you do not agree, do not be pulled into an argument. Say things like, 'Your view is interesting' (the word 'interesting' works wonders) or, 'Hmm, let us move on. Who else would like to make a point?'

What if they say, 'But I am asking you'? Reflect your deep desire to find out what their view is. Otherwise throw open to the whole audience again. Someone somewhere will have a viewpoint. And if they do not, say, 'No one seems interested in that point. Let us move on.' Again you could ask them to see you later to discuss it further – if you can cope with the questioner.

Some audiences need to test the speaker. Do not waffle, lie or avoid an honest answer. The techniques above should still serve you well.

After presentations you are sometimes required to manage a discussion. There are some tips to help with this:

HANDLING

DISCUSSIONS

● Have some questions prepared to start the audience off. Show them the questions in some form, using visual aids.

51

- Ask a question and wait at least 10 seconds longer than you usually feel comfortable with. Someone else will fill the silence. Don't be afraid of silence. It is thinking time for the audience as well as you.
- Break the audience into pairs or groups. Ask them to think about the presentation and find a question to ask the other pairs or groups. Then let them ask it.
- Repeat the question asked by someone else so that the audience can hear it and respond. You are facing the audience but someone close to the front may have their back to others.
- To end the discussion, summarize the key points made by the audience.

STEPS TO KEEP YOUR VOICE NATURAL

- Cut down on throat clearing and coughing.
- Avoid shouting.
- Pitch your voice at a level that is easy for you.
- Vary pace and tone so you sound interesting.
- Pause for breath.
- Avoid smoking or excessive alcohol as these have an adverse effect on the voice.
- Have water to sip.

COPING WITH ANXIETY

Tick the items as you go. They will help you to order your thinking before a presentation or speech and chase away some of your anxiety. It is always worth remembering that some 'nerves' are good for you. It gives you enough adrenalin to carry you through.

- I will organize my material well in advance, so that on the day I only need to review it.
- I will have checked that my topic is what is wanted and has the right focus.
- I will know who my audience is.
- I will have ordered the equipment I need and know who to contact if:
  - it isn't there; or
  - it isn't working.
- I will be reasonably familiar with the venue – or will arrive early to become so.
- I will visualize myself making a good presentation where all goes well.

- I will have rehearsed using all my visual aids.
- I will breathe deeply before I go on.
- I will release tension in a positive way – by walking about (but not pacing) or thinking about something else for 10 minutes or sitting quietly by myself.
- I will stay relaxed and natural whilst I speak, being very familiar with my material and moving when I speak.
- I will not rely on scripts but have some notecards or visual aids to keep me on track.
- I will maintain good eye contact with my audience and greet them.

WORKPIECE 3.10

PRESENTATION – YOUR ACTION PLAN

Make a list of areas you wish to work on and an action plan for how you will move forward:

I need to work on ...

How I will do it ...

CHECKLIST

- Be confident and know your material.
- Assume that the audience wants you to do well.
- Be yourself.
- Practise the techniques for relieving pre-presentation nerves.
- Presentations can be fun. They are a good way to communicate with large groups of people. Using these techniques will help you to convey positive and confident presentations.

The following section considers personal skills that you can develop to help you cope with the demands of a new or changing environment. If you manage your time, you find that there seems to be more of it to do what you need to do and what you want to do. If you can cope with the stresses of a fast-moving and demanding world you will be healthier and happier.

**TIME MANAGEMENT
SKILLS**

No matter what profession you enter, what job you do or how you spend your time at work or at leisure, you have precisely 24 hours each day, seven days each week and 52 weeks each year.

How you spend the time is important and it has been estimated that at work we are effective for only 30–40% of our time. Does this mean we are wasting at least 60% of the time available to us?

Before starting to consider techniques to manage time we need to analyse how we spend it now. We hurry from deadline to deadline; rush from place to place; hoard our reading until we have too much to face at once; leave no space for our research; work into the early hours to finalize an assignment; and find ways to take shortcuts so that we have more time to waste time.

In the built environment professions time is spent in meetings, making plans, agreeing deadlines – and sometimes it feels as if there is no time to do the actual tasks we have to do: talking to clients; responding to their needs; writing that report; producing an award-winning design; estimating the quantities of material needed; looking at a site; interviewing tenants and prospective tenants; devising the strategy for the future planning needs of the local authority, or whatever constitutes the profession we have chosen. We may also find that life outside our work begins to suffer. Where is the time to read a novel, play a sport, take up or continue with a hobby, meet our friends or spend relaxed time with our families?

In this section we consider what you can do to begin to take control of your time and your life. This is developed further in Chapter 10.

PLAN FOR YOUR LIFE

Set your goals. You need to take some time to think about where you are now and what you want to do in your life.

MAKE A LIST OF YOUR LIFETIME GOALS

Remember that you are not writing them in stone and no one needs to see them except you, so you can be as ambitious or as modest in your goals as you wish. They are for you.

REVIEW YOUR GOALS REGULARLY

Review where you are as often as you wish, but it helps to know where you are heading. Certainly it is a common question in an interview for a job: 'Where do you see yourself in 5 years', 10 years' time?' Too often we find this difficult to answer because we never take the time to consider it.

SET YOUR PRIORITIES   Use 'A' for your most important goals, 'B' for your next most important, 'C' for your least important (or most impractical) goals. Goals will change and you can move them from B or C priority to A priority over time.

PLAN YOUR STRATEGIES   Goals cannot be 'done', they are not tasks, so the next step is to plan what you can do to achieve your goals. Take each one and think about what you are going to do to move yourself towards that goal. You don't have to get there all at once, but can plan to achieve something to move you forward.

CHECKLIST
- Set your goals.
- List your priorities.
- Plan your strategies.

All this is useful but what can you do to organize what you are doing now, at work, at home or in your leisure time? The first thing that setting goals does is help you to see if what you are doing now is what you really want or need to do with your time and for the rest of your life. But let's go back to the day to day.

CONSIDER YOUR PERSONAL TIME BANDITS   Reflect on what you achieved yesterday, last week, last month. Why do you need to tell yourself you work better under pressure when you leave that assignment until the night before it is due to be handed in, or you only think about that presentation five minutes before you stand up? What are you spending your time on?

PLAN YOUR TIME   You need to establish what you want to achieve in the time available. Write down everything that needs to be done. Consider the envelope of time available after known commitments are taken into account. What can you achieve in that time?

ESTIMATE YOUR TIMINGS   Allow for some extra tasks if you move through your list more quickly than you anticipate. But over- rather than under-estimate your timings. You can always find another task if you finish earlier!

ESTABLISH YOUR PRIORITIES   Use letters, numbers or stars to denote your order of importance. For example:

A = Must do today.
B = Should be done today.
C = Might be done today.

Complete all A-priority tasks. Do this before moving on to Bs, then all Bs before moving to Cs. If you can't complete all of a task, make notes of what needs doing so that you can return to it as soon as possible.

BE FLEXIBLE   The priority list is a guide or tool to help you work more effectively. It is not a new kind of tyrant. In the face of changes, keep asking: 'What matters now?'

Transfer tasks not completed on to a new list. Do this at the end of each day. This saves time the following morning and implies commitment to getting the task done. It also helps you to clear your head of things 'running around' in it overnight.

Are you transferring items from one list to the next? Ask yourself why. Is it too difficult or too large a task? If it is, break it down into smaller 'chunks' and tackle one chunk at a time.

CHECKLIST
- Consider your personal time bandits.
- Plan your time.
- Estimate your timings.
- Establish your priorities.
- Complete 'A' tasks first.
- Be flexible.
- Ask: 'What matters now?'

MANAGING TASKS

CREATE BLOCKS OF UNINTERRUPTED TIME   Look at your personal time clock and decide which is your most effective time. This could be at the beginning or end of the day, before or after work. Pick out the most important item to be tackled, your 'A' task. How much of it can you accomplish in the time available?

KEEP IT INTERESTING   Intersperse dull tasks with more interesting ones to keep you going. Intersperse active work with more passive tasks. Batch similar tasks together.

MANAGEABLE CHUNKS   If you have a major task or assignment, an 'A' task, divide it into smaller tasks or chunks. Intersperse with other tasks to keep both your interest and to keep it fresh. This also makes the task easier to tackle as it no longer seems quite so daunting.

USE ALL YOUR TIME EFFECTIVELY   If you have only a short amount of time available, do something to move the 'A' task along: read an article or chapter for information; plan the next stage in brief notes or headings; draw a quick mind map.

CHECKLIST
● Create blocks of uninterrupted time.
● Keep it interesting.
● Manageable chunks.
● Use all your time effectively.

WORK WHERE YOU WILL NOT BE EASILY DISTURBED
How is your working space organized? If you face a wall or partition whilst you are working, rather than facing out into the room, you can be more focused. People are less likely to disturb you.

ORGANIZE YOUR SPACE   Have only the work you are dealing with in front of you. Having prioritized the rest, tuck it away so that it does not distract you. Do you have enough workspace to put away or to one side what you are not working on at the moment? Have you sufficient desk or table space, drawers, shelves, etc.? Is there anything you can do about this?

TOOLS   Have your necessary tools at hand on your desk or easily available – for example, in your top drawer. You shouldn't need to be searching for a pen, ruler, paper clip, post-its or a notepad.

TIDY UP WHEN YOU FINISH   Tidy your workspace each time you leave for more than one hour, and certainly before finishing work for the day. Remember to end your day by reviewing your tasks for the following working session.

CHECKLIST
● Work where you will not be disturbed.
● Organize your space.
● Have the necessary tools at hand.
● Tidy up when you finish.

**ORGANIZE YOUR
WORKSPACE**

These techniques should go part of the way to helping you to manage the time you have available more effectively. If you can take control of your time, you are in control of your life and your future.

SUMMARY

We can all improve or develop our existing skills. By so doing we should become more effective in the ways we work. We should, by being able to manage our activities better, improve our abilities to work with and manage others. This is not to suggest that we should improve all our personal skills at once. Rather, these skills should be developed over time by the Kolb approach of plan, action and review. The craftsman, whose work we may admire, will have spent many years developing his skills. So it is with our personal and self-management skills.

FURTHER READING

Garrett, S. (1985) *Manage Your Time*, Fontana.

Janner, G. (1989) *Janner on Presentations*, 2nd edn, Business Books.

Mondel, S. (1989) *Effective Presentation Skills*, 2nd edn, Kogan Page.

Murphy, E. and Snell, S. (1992) *Effective Writing*, Pitman.

Sussams, J.E. (1986) *How to Write Effective Reports*, Gower.

PART TWO

LEARNING HOW TO BUILD AND WORK IN TEAMS

WORKING IN TEAMS

GEOFF CROOK AND MIKE WATERHOUSE

For many built environment practitioners and students a significant amount of time is spent working in teams. This team-work may involve a wide range of activities including information sharing, problem solving and decision making. Some of the teams we work with are more effective than others. Simply bringing together practitioners with the required range of skills and professional expertise does not in itself guarantee that a team will work well. Nor does it mean that the outputs will be of high quality.

The patterns of behaviour which occur within a team can directly affect performance. This chapter discusses the characteristics of effective teams and introduces models of team development. It examines ways in which people behave in teams and pays particular attention to the roles of team leader and chair. These ideas are developed further in Chapters 5 and 6.

After reading this chapter you should be able to:

- describe the characteristics of effective teams;

- discuss the relationships between task needs and process needs in team working;

- consider models of team development;

- consider how behavioural characteristics of people might influence team building;

- discuss what might be required of team leaders or chairs.

INTRODUCTION

We may all be familiar with teams such as the design and build team, the project team, the housing management team, the local plans team or the estate management team.

Some teams may be set up to carry out a specific task and may have a temporary existence (e.g. the project management team for a design and build project; a working group to report on the condition of housing association stock). Other teams may not have any formal status but may be informal groupings or networks of people. These may simply occur because people feel a need to share information and test out ideas. Team or group working can involve a wide range of activities including information collecting and sharing, problem solving, ideas testing, decision making, professional support, networking and socializing. However, simply putting groups of practitioners or students together does not in itself create teams which are effective. Many factors affect the way in which teams operate and the extent to which they can become effective. Such factors might include:

- the different personalities involved;
- the patterns of behaviour within the group;
- the different value systems of individuals and professions;
- the nature of the organization within which the team is operating;
- the nature of the work or of the task;
- the educational background and experience of different individuals.

Given such a range of factors it is not surprising that many teams do not realize their full potential and sometimes waste time in needless argument or activity. This chapter, together with Chapters 5 and 6, is about how individuals within teams may improve their performance.

GROUPS AND TEAMS

Groups can be defined as two or more individuals who interact with one another and where there is a psychological interrelationship between them.[1] Six people waiting at a bus stop on a wet day may not constitute a group. But if the bus comes late, sprays them with water and does not stop, then they may become a 'group' in their resolve to communicate their feelings to the bus company. A group may form and define itself, for example an action group set up to oppose the building of an airport or a motorway.

For a group to exist there must be a significant level of interdependence between individuals to the extent that members perceive the group to be real and to the extent that members can readily distinguish themselves from non-members.[1]

An example is a sports team which identifies itself through its team colours. With such a team, members take on specific roles or tasks and these too are recognized by the group as a whole. Such roles build in expectations of behaviour from individuals (e.g. a goal keeper will try to stop the ball going into the net).

The terms 'group' and 'team' have no clear or universal definition and tend to be used interchangeably. Generally, however, the meaning of the word team is taken to infer a higher order of interdependence and cooperation between members than is found in a group. In addition the achievement of some degree of 'synergy' is usually implied by the word team. With synergy the combination of the differing strengths of team members is seen as producing an output which exceeds the sum of the outputs of individuals.

Book 1 of this series (*Collaborative Practice in the Built Environment*) describes how the construction and development industry has responded to the increasing complexity of issues. Part of this response has been an increasing use of working groups and teams which bring together a wide range of professional knowledge and expertise. The costs of group working, however, are high. In order to remain cost effective it is essential that these groups develop quickly into effective teams and achieve high levels of synergy.

EXAMPLE

The members of the Parish Council of the ancient and beautiful village of Much Haddock recently met to express their concern over the future of a mediaeval barn which is in poor condition. This barn is a large building of considerable historical and architectural interest. It is located in a prominent position in the village. Adjacent to the barn is an overgrown traditional water meadow and adjoining it is a badly managed ancient woodland.

The District Council wishes to apply for a grant to restore part of the building. It hopes to find an economic use for the barn and to provide for the future management of the water meadow and woodland. It decides that it needs the advice of a group of experts.

In this example it is unlikely that it would be possible to find any one person who could offer all the advice needed. The task needs a wide range of professional expertise and experience. This is typical of many built environment projects. The example suggests that it is important for any professional to have an understanding of the types of skill required (for a particular task) to put together a team with relevant experience. In practice people forming a team may come from a number of backgrounds and professions.

WORKPIECE 4.1

ADVICE TO THE PARISH COUNCIL

In the example outlined for Much Haddock, consider what advice you could give to the Parish Council as to the range of knowledge, skills and expertise that may be required. List these in order of priority.

THE CHARACTERISTICS OF EFFECTIVE TEAMS

When we bring together a group of individuals, whose range of skills, knowledge and expertise fully meet the specific requirements of a task, what prospect is there that this team would work well and be successful? Some groups of people with similar skills and experience perform better than others. What other factors can there be which influence how effectively a group of people can work together? One way of exploring this is to consider some of the teams we know ourselves. We may be able to learn from any team, whether successful or not. Do not read any further until you have done Workpiece 4.2.

WORKPIECE 4.2

MEMBERSHIP OF A TEAM

Consider any team which you have been a member of or which you know about.

- What do you think helped to make it effective?
- What do you think made it less effective?

From our research with many teams of people working in the built environment, we would suggest that the characteristics of an effective team could include:

- a range of professional, functional or other expertise, knowledge and experience necessary for carrying out a task;
- a clear understanding of the task and a strong commitment to its completion;
- a structure and organization agreed by or acceptable to the team members;

- a way of improving the team's activities by learning from its experiences;
- a clear communication system;
- a high level of participation by members of the team.

What is clear from this kind of list is that successful teams have attributes which go beyond technical and professional expertise and experience.

WORKPIECE 4.3

CHARACTERISTICS OF AN EFFECTIVE TEAM

From your experience, would you like to add to this list?
Usually characters are prioritized. Do you think this would be useful in this case?

TEAM NEEDS, INDIVIDUAL NEEDS AND COMPLETING THE TASK

John Adair suggests[2] that a team has three main areas of concern:

- completion of the task;
- meeting the needs of individuals within the team;
- enabling the team to work together (maintaining the team).

The three areas of need are often illustrated diagrammatically as interlocking circles (Figure 4.1). This is meant to imply that these three areas are self-reinforcing and that to neglect one or more will reduce the overall strength of the team. In other words the possible level of synergy within the team will be reduced.

Obviously the task and its completion are the main concern of any team. When a stage of that task is completed (e.g. a tender document is

Figure 4.1 Adair's 'Three Areas of Need'.

submitted, the presentation of a scheme to a client is finished) there may be self-congratulation and celebration by the team. However, whilst there are still stages of the task to be completed a tension tends to remain in teams. Adair emphasizes the need to develop and maintain working relationships among team members whilst the team still has work to do.

Unlike the task, which is usually seen in terms of things rather than people, group maintenance is primarily about people and how they relate to each other as they work on the group task. For example, the team of practitioners involved in preparing alternative solutions for the barn in Much Haddock (Workpiece 1.1) would need to share information and to draw out ideas and suggestions from the team in order to build and create solutions.

Adair further describes how individuals bring their own needs with them into a group. A team can represent an opportunity for fulfilling individual needs. In fact we sometimes join a team for this purpose. It may be a route to developing experience, to building self-esteem or to receiving respect from colleagues. The model put forward by Adair suggests that 'if the group and individual needs can be met along with, and not at the expense of, the group task then the group will tend to be more effective'. We shall look at this further in Chapter 5.

CHARACTERISTICS AND STAGES OF TEAM DEVELOPMENT

Research suggests that some groups develop and become teams. A number of researchers have tried to identify and classify the stages that groups may go through as they progress to become teams. We shall look at two models.

FORMING, STORMING, NORMING AND PERFORMING

The first model suggests four stages: forming, storming, norming and performing.[2]

STAGE 1 – FORMING At this stage the group members are uncertain about what to do and how to work together. There is a tendency for them to follow any suggestion which seems sensible and will often play 'follow my leader'. Usually there is little positive interaction between group members and very little concern for each other's working or personal problems. Members may be hesitant to commit themselves to the work of the group. Some, however, may be over-anxious to commit themselves because they perceive that potentially the work of the group could be important to them.

STAGE 2 – STORMING As the name suggests this stage may be characterized by discussion or even argument about the nature of the job to be done, how to do it and what needs to be done. In so doing members of the group may listen more carefully to what others have to say and may also show a greater concern for the difficulties or problems faced by their colleagues. Some groups never progress beyond this stage.

STAGE 3 – NORMING Now the group is beginning to settle down and become a team. It has a greater understanding of the task and starts to establish ways of working. It can start to be effective by planning and organizing itself to complete the task. As the group becomes a team it now starts to show real concern for the needs of individuals and the group (Figures 4.2 and 4.3).

- How do we ensure that the contributions of individuals are recognized and acknowledged?
- How will personal problems in relation to the task be identified?
- How can individuals learn to work as a team?
- How can 'difficult' individuals be handled?

Figure 4.2 Individual needs.

- How can team spirit be built/developed?
- How can the team be best motivated and encouraged?
- How can good communication be developed and maintained between members of the team?
- Does the team have any particular training needs?
- How can team discipline and professionalism be maintained?
- How can relationships between other groups or organizations outside the team be maintained?

Figure 4.3 Group needs.

STAGE 4 – PERFORMING Now the group is operating at its maximum level of effectiveness and is making the best use of its resources. Members are able to work very flexibly and leadership may become unnecessary. As a team it will feel very cohesive and will concern itself with aspects of its members' needs as well as work. The team will also try to develop deeper understanding of the needs of individuals in the group and will try to develop means of ensuring that those needs are met.

Not all groups go through all of these stages. Many groups never get beyond the forming stage. Others get to the storming stage and spend so much time in argument and discussion that they either disintegrate and become totally ineffective or leave themselves very little time to complete the task. Some groups may produce quite credible outputs despite their inability to reach a performing stage, but this is likely to reflect the abilities of one or two individuals rather than the output of a truly collaborative team effort.

CHAOTIC, FORMAL AND SKILLED

Another model identifies three stages viz: chaotic, formal and skilled.[3]

THE CHAOTIC STAGE   A group could be said to be at the 'chaotic' stage when, despite a lot of time and energy being expended, achievement tends to be low. Groups at this stage often try to make up for uncertainty by throwing themselves with vigour into each activity. However, they tend to do this without stopping to discuss exactly what the task is. They simply do what some members think is the task.

At this chaotic stage the group:

- makes up for uncertainty by throwing itself into each activity;
- devotes little attention to agreeing objectives;
- gives insufficient time to planning how to tackle the task;
- has no appointed leader or a leader whose role is unclear (attempts by a leader to exert authority are likely to be rejected by members);
- generates ideas but wastes most of them (lack of listening or structure for debate).

Such a group is only likely to achieve patchy success and may not even be able to sustain this if it remains at the chaotic stage.

THE FORMAL STAGE   Groups at the 'formal' stage tend to begin imposing order on the way they work but in doing so they become over-formal. They may now know more clearly what they are doing and where they want to go – but they concentrate on working to the rules, at the expense of accomplishing the task.

A group at this formal stage:

- has rigid procedures for objective setting and planning;

- demands strong leadership – which is seen as the answer to the uncertainty and problems of the earlier stages of chaos;
- finds scapegoats – particularly by blaming difficulties on:
  - the leader's failure to control the group;
  - the nature of the task;
  - the brief;
  - people's non-observance of the procedures;
- assigns people specific jobs, such as time-keeper and secretary, and expects them to stick to those jobs.

Such a group may sometimes succeed – but only when there is time for the task to be completed, despite all the procedures it feels must be carried out.

THE SKILLED STAGE Groups are said to be at the 'skilled' stage when the team has learned the flexibility needed to complete tasks effectively.

At this stage groups begin to understand that the alternative to chaos need not be the strict adherence to rules – rather they need to review the rules continually, and be prepared to challenge and adapt them if certain formalities are inappropriate for the task in hand.

A group at this skilled stage:

- has flexible procedures for objective setting and planning;
- has a leader who is more supportive than directive (and may often feel redundant as the group frequently seems not to need leading);
- shares responsibility and recognition for its successes;
- works in an atmosphere of trust and cooperation.

A group functioning at the skilled stage is likely to be very effective. With careful leadership a group can become a team. A team is a group with a difference – it is a higher level, more cohesive gathering of people than any of the groups outlined so far in this model.

COMPARING THE MODELS

These models, although they have similarities, perhaps illustrate the stages through which two different types of team might progress. The first model (Forming, etc.) is perhaps closest to the work team which has been put together on the basis of professional expertise, status and experience. Typically this team will have been given a 'leader' or chair.

Examples of such teams might be a local plans team, a design and build team, a housing management team.

The second model (Chaos, etc.) is perhaps closest to the kinds of team which are assembled to give a range of professional expertise but where status is not seen as necessarily important and it is up to the team itself to sort out its 'leadership' or chair. The team assembled to solve the problem of Much Haddock in our earlier example perhaps illustrates this. So too are teams of students from different professions working together on assignments.

WORKPIECE 4.4

STAGES OF TEAM DEVELOPMENT

Think again of a team you have been in, or seen in operation. Can you identify at what stage it might have been in either of the two models?

Perhaps you can trace the team's progress through these stages.

A major issue for a team to address at a very early stage in their formation, therefore, is how they can work at their team working. This is important if teams are to avoid spending too much time 'forming and storming' or in 'chaos and formality' resulting in disillusionment and even the collapse of the team itself. We discuss this further in Chapter 5 and suggest ways of getting started.

PEOPLE IN TEAMS

We are all different. Furthermore our behaviour in a group may be different from our behaviour as an individual. We have already identified that the way people behave in a team may have a significant bearing on that team's performance. Let us try and analyse this further. A great deal of research has been directed at the roles which individuals may take within a team. We can describe these as behavioural roles – for example, chair, team worker or ideas person – which reflect particular personal characteristics. A way of identifying these roles is suggested by Belbin.[4] His research identified eight key roles (Figure 4.4).

One way of assembling a team would be on the basis of Belbin's behavioural roles. In the built environment, teams are usually assembled on the basis of professional backgrounds but role playing can be a very useful exercise for a team of people who do not know each other well. It can certainly be helpful in any early 'getting to know you' phase. Often when people are being replaced in teams the search for their replace-

Type	Symbol	Typical features	Positive qualities	Allowable weaknesses
Company worker	CW	Conservative, dutiful, predictable.	Organizing ability, practical common sense, hard-working, self-discipline.	Lack of flexibility, unresponsiveness to unproven ideas.
Chairman	CH	Calm, self-confident, controlled.	A capacity for treating and welcoming all potential contributors on their merits and without prejudice. A strong sense of objectives.	No more than ordinary in terms of intellect or creative ability.
Shaper	SH	Highly strung, outgoing, dynamic.	Drive and a readiness to challenge inertia, ineffectiveness, complacency or self-deception.	Proneness to provocation, irritation and impatience.
Plant	PL	Individualistic, serious-minded, unorthodox.	Genius, imagination, intellect, knowledge.	Up in the clouds, inclined to disregard practical details or protocol.
Resource investigator	RI	Extroverted, enthusiastic, curious, communicative.	A capacity for contacting people and exploring anything new. An ability to respond to challenge.	Liable to lose interest once the initial fascination has passed.
Monitor–evaluator	ME	Sober, unemotional, prudent.	Judgement, discretion, hard-headedness.	Lacks inspiration or the ability to motivate others.
Team worker	TW	Socially orientated, rather mild, sensitive.	An ability to respond to people and to situations, and to promote team spirit.	Indecisiveness at moments of crisis.
Completer–finisher	CF	Painstaking, orderly, conscientious, anxious.	A capacity for follow-through. Perfectionism.	A tendency to worry about small things. A reluctance to 'let go'.

Figure 4.4 Behaviour roles in teams (from Belbin[4])

WORKPIECE 4.5

BELBIN QUESTIONNAIRE

You might like to complete Belbin's questionnaire (in Belbin, 1981[4]) and identify your strongest inherent natural roles.

ment will involve a consideration of their role contribution. Given two professionals with more or less equal ranges of experience, it could well be a key factor in making the choice.

(Note that psychometric tests or behavioural questionnaires need to be interpreted with caution. They are generalized guides and should not be taken as absolutes for all time. For example, many people who come high as company workers/team workers often perform well as chairs with experience and training.)

Belbin suggests that an effective team would normally cover all eight of these roles. The suggestion is that if a team has not got some-one who is a natural as chair, for example, then a team member may have to play that role. The team may also devise a strategy to help the chair to play this role. Similarly if a team has not got a natural 'completer finisher' it may be useful for the team to ask (coerce!) someone to undertake that specific role. Alternatively a team may have too many 'shapers' or 'monitor evaluators'. It may well be in the team's interest for those members to play down their natural inclinations and play up other characteristics which may be more useful to their team. For example, you may contribute a really good idea at the beginning of the team's work. That does not mean that you have fulfilled your role in relation to the team! We all have to act as team workers if everything necessary to complete a task is to be done effectively.

Whether or not a team can take decisions collaboratively may depend upon leadership style within it. Some teams may be free to influence how decisions are made and to choose to operate collaboratively. Others may have an appointed leader but still may choose to operate in a collaborative style. These issues are discussed in Chapter 6.

CHAIRING THE TEAM

The chair is usually a key role in ensuring that team meetings are effective and hence is worth looking at in detail. The role of chair in team meetings is often poorly understood by participants and is often confused with concepts of leadership, dynamic personalities and so on. Equally people are often elected, 'volunteered' or press-ganged into chairing team meetings without any form of training or advice in this important team role.

For some teams, chairs are automatically selected by their position in the hierarchy of the organization, e.g. the leader of a local plans section would expect to chair meetings of a local plans team and the housing director in a housing association would expect to chair meetings of teams considering tenant selection policy. Obviously in many cases this is both logical and correct but it may not always be the best choice. This confuses two ideas: those of status and role. The two can be in conflict. Figure 4.5 takes a closer look at what a chair is expected to do; Figure 4.6 offers some tips.

An effective chair:
- enables the team to define possible outcomes;
- ensures that all members understand the issues they are discussing;
- tries to prevent misunderstandings and confusion;
- tries to encourage participation by all team members;
- tries to maintain the unity/cohesiveness of the team;
- ensures that the meeting is conducted properly;
- ensures that the meeting follows the 'rules'.

Figure 4.5 Role of an effective chair.

DO	DO NOT
• Start the meeting on time	• Allow separate discussions to develop during the meeting
• Agree a finishing time and stick to it if you can (2 hours should be long enough – even if this means deferring some items to the next time)	• Allow one member to hog the discussion; stop them and encourage others to make a contribution
• Make sure everyone can see and hear you (and you can see and hear them!)	• Take sides in a debate or discussion
• Have an agenda, agree the order and stick to it (!!) and ensure everyone has one	• Let debates/arguments move from the issues into personal comments
• Take short 'comfort breaks' if the meeting is necessarily going to be long	• Reprimand members of the team in the meeting; this is unfair as they may have no opportunity to defend themselves
• Keep discussions to the point	• Let the powerful outspoken personalities dominate: bring in the quiet personalities – they may have something very interesting to offer.
• Bring everyone into the discussion – by going round the group one by one if necessary	
• Recognize the signs of boredom or people ceasing to take part in the meeting	
• Try to summarize the main points of a discussion – and seek agreement to the accuracy of your summary ('Have I got it right?') before moving on	
• Put decisions to a vote if there has been adequate discussion; if there are difficulties in doing this it may be opportune to take the temperature of the meeting by asking members how they would vote (also known as a 'straw vote')	
• Ensure that discussions and the actions necessary to carry them out are recorded.	

Figure 4.6 Tips for the chair!

Not surprisingly, not everyone makes a good chairperson. Perhaps we should note that although some of the roles are similar to those of a 'leader', leadership itself is not expected in a chair – and sometimes can be a disadvantage. This is often a problem for students working on group/team projects or other groups where all members are equal in status – the collaborative task team referred to earlier. In these cases there can be a temptation to select or elect as chair the person who speaks the loudest and seems to know what they are doing or know what is required from the project or task. This can lead to disaster and often results in the chair being replaced late into the project. The selection of a chair needs to be done with great care. A Belbin-type questionnaire may help to indicate those people in the team who are the most likely candidates. Utilizing this kind of questionnaire, whilst not perfect, helps to give a greater objectivity and could help to remove some sensitive personal issues. (Look back at the characteristics of a chair identified by Belbin.)

Some teams may opt for a cooperative style of operation without specifically identifying a chair. In practice this style is difficult to sustain for long periods and usually a team adopts a 'chair-like' approach in the end. Other teams may adopt a system of rotating the chairs systematically between all the team members. This allows different team members the opportunity to experience the chairing role which may be important to individuals in their personal development.

SUSPENDING BUSINESS

When a group is in difficulty or recognizes that it is not being effective, a technique which can be useful is 'suspending business'. As the name implies, this technique involves the group withdrawing from all the tasks in hand and reflecting upon what is happening. The following are examples of the sorts of question a team might ask of itself:

- What is going on in the group?
  - What are the pre-occupations of the group?
  - What problems are the group facing?
  - Do members tend to operate as pairs or other minority groupings?
  - What roles are members playing?
- What are the feelings within the group about what is going on?
  - Can the group identify examples of helpful and unhelpful behaviour?
  - Who tends to contribute the most; and the least?
- What have we learnt so far?

- What do we know about the values and attitudes of individual members of the group?
- Do any of our reflections suggest that we might change the way we do things?

SUMMARY

Effective teams appear to exhibit common characteristics which go beyond the accumulation of skills, experience and professional expertise of its members and include behavioural aspects such as cooperation, participation, commitment and cohesiveness. The old adage, 'Know thyself,' applies as much to teams as it does to individuals.

According to Adair, teams are more likely to be effective if they are able to meet the needs of the task, the team and of the individual.

A number of models have been put forward to explain the stages of team development. These may have value for teams in understanding what is happening to themselves. It may also have a value in 'suspending business' etc.

The roles of team leader and chair are often poorly understood yet can be critical to the effective performance of teams.

CHECKLIST OF POINTS

- What characteristics tend to be common in effective teams?
- What actions might you consider taking in meeting each of Adair's 'Three Team Needs'?
- Outline a model which describes the stages of team development.
- Suggest questions which a team might ask of itself in suspending business.
- What behavioural roles might you expect to find in an effective team?
- What characteristics would you expect of an effective or chair?

REFERENCES

1. Wilson, C. and Rosenfeld, R.H. (1990) *Managing Organisations*, McGraw-Hill, London.
2. Adair, J. (1986) *Effective Team Building*, Gower.
3. British Petroleum (1992) *BP Training Manual*.
4. Belbin, R.M. (1981) *Management Teams*, Heinemann.

FURTHER READING

Hirschonn, L. (1991) *Managing in the New Team Environment*, Addison-Wesley, Reading, Mass.
Janner, G. (1986) *Janner on Meetings*, Gower.

Larson, C. and La Fasto, F. (1989) *Teamwork*, Sage.

Moxon, E. (1993) *Building a Better Team*, Gower.

Seymour-Smith, L. (1984) *Making Your Meetings More Effective*, Management Update Ltd.

Tropman, H.E. (1981) *Effective Meetings*, 2nd edn, Sage.

Video Arts (1976) *Meetings, Bloody Meetings*.

TEAMS IN ACTION

GEOFF CROOK AND MIKE WATERHOUSE

It is our experience that many of the problems encountered by teams in a built environment context stem from their initial approaches to the task. This chapter builds on Chapter 4 and examines ways in which teams might approach these first crucial stages in order to maximize effectiveness.

THEME

By the end of this chapter you should be able to:

OBJECTIVES

● explore, using examples, some of the difficulties of getting started;

● explore a methodical approach to getting started;

● examine the issues involved in defining a task, in planning and organizing a team, in examining resource requirements and in considering the needs of both individuals and teams;

● explore ways of planning, organizing, conducting and reporting on team meetings.

We are going to consider two groups of students who have been given a task that involves producing proposals for a hall of residence on a site located on a university campus. The groups, which include students from courses in quantity surveying, town planning, landscape architecture, architecture, building surveying, estate management, engineering and housing studies, are briefed on the task and meet as groups for the first time.

INTRODUCTION

GROUP A

FIRST MEETING, WEEK 1   This proved to be a friendly, busy group, full of enthusiasm and energy. The first meeting began with a brief exchange of views about what the task might mean.

Discussion quickly turned to options and solutions, which flowed quite freely from each member of the team. Different opinions were voiced about which were the best ideas, with some team members strongly defending their own suggestions. The team found it difficult to reach agreement and the general feeling was that the team was getting nowhere.

One member suggested that they should look again at the brief and try and identify criteria to test out all the options. The group accepted this idea and each option was assessed against a range of criteria. The first meeting ended with everyone agreeing to one solution. A decision was taken that each group member would explore this solution further in time for the next meeting.

WORKPIECE 5.1

A TEAM IN 'CHAOS'

The individual members of Group A are enthusiastic and full of ideas. They had difficulty in reaching agreement as to whose was the best idea.

What difficulties can you foresee for this group?

WEEKS 2 AND 3   The group continued to work over several weeks. Each member returned to the next meeting with further ideas; some had clearly carried out background research, others had explored design solutions. The team struggled with these different contributions. After a lengthy period of discussion a decision emerged which involved giving individuals responsibility for part of the task and dividing the work between subgroups.

The team decided to elect a chairperson. Subgroups were set up to carry out specific tasks and a chair was also elected for each subgroup. It was decided that subgroup chairs would be responsible for monitoring progress and reporting back to a steering group. Rules about attendance and meeting deadlines were agreed. A lengthy discussion followed about how to ensure that everyone would make a fair and reasonable contribution to the task.

In week 3, despite spending over four hours at its weekly group meeting, the group failed to address all the items on the agenda. The meeting only finished because most members had drifted away.

Group A has spent much of its time and energies in planning, organizing and controlling its activities. It has made progress but the processes it has evolved appear to be rigid and time consuming. This inefficiency in the group's use of time may seriously impair its effectiveness in reaching a successful completion of the task.

This group may succeed but only if there is sufficient time for the task to be completed, despite all the procedures which must be carried out.

GROUP B

FIRST MEETING, WEEK 1 In this group three people quickly engaged in a discussion about their experiences of student accommodation and what students might see as the ideal hall of residence. Two members focused upon the brief and had a lively discussion about what the task meant. The remaining members of this group listened to these discussions but added very little; at times their attention drifted and they talked about other things.

Towards the end of this meeting it was suggested that the group needed a leader and one member of the group, who stated that she now had a much clearer idea about the task, was asked to be the group leader. No one disagreed.

WORKPIECE 5.2

GROUP PARTICIPATION

Some members appear to be developing a view about what the task means but this view is not necessarily shared by the group as a whole.

- What difficulties can you foresee in this for the group?
- Suggest ways in which the group might explore the requirements of the brief and promote a shared understanding.

During this meeting some members took little part in discussions about the project.

- Suggest a range of different reasons as to why this may have happened.
- What action might the group take to improve group participation in meetings?

WEEKS 2 AND 3 At their next meeting, the group leader arrived with a schedule showing the dates when key tasks were to be completed. The group started to discuss the schedule. One member suggested that it was more important to get on with the job and the meeting ended soon after.

In week 3, concern was expressed about the lack of real progress. Some members strongly resented this criticism because they had spent many hours on tasks that were identified in the schedule. Other members were critical of the plan as a whole and began to blame the leader; they said that two weeks had been wasted doing the wrong things.

A heated debate ensued about the nature of the task. Some members expressed the view that the brief was inadequate. A vote was taken and a new leader was elected.

Group B has experienced a serious setback. It saw leadership as an answer to its initial problems of a lack of clear objectives and commitment. However, the leader's authority to set a direction and organize the group was challenged; individuals within the group began looking for scapegoats to blame for lack of progress. Agreement within the group as a whole had not been reached, either about the requirements of the brief or about the objectives of the group.

WORKPIECE 5.3

STAGES OF TEAM DEVELOPMENT

Read through again the account of the progress made by the two student groups. (Refer back to Chapter 4 – models of team development.)

- What stage of development do you think that each group has reached?

- What advice could you give to Group A to help in its development?
- What actions might you consider taking if you were the newly appointed leader of Group B?

The examples of Groups A and B illustrate how teams of similar expertise and experience can approach the same task in quite difference ways. Some teams learn from their experiences and develop quickly, others do not.

GETTING STARTED – A METHODICAL APPROACH

Figure 5.1 illustrates an approach which some teams might find useful. The model suggests that there are six areas which a team needs to address at the outset and throughout the life of the task. The first step is to define the task (Figure 5.2). The model also suggests that the areas interact and indicates what is possible within the constraints of the team itself and available time and resources.

The processes of discussion or debate involved in addressing these kinds of question may highlight the differences in value sets held by the different built environment professionals. In the example of Much Haddock (Chapter 4), each of the professions could have a particular set of concerns. An architect could view this problem as presenting a series of design opportunities; a planner could be concerned with what the peo-

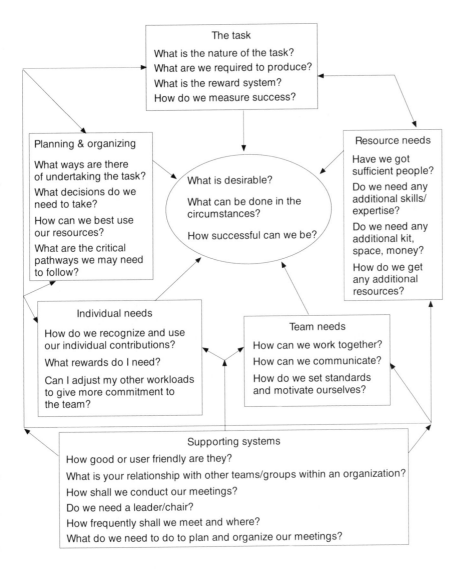

The task

What is the nature of the task?
What are we required to produce?
What is the reward system?
How do we measure success?

Planning & organizing

What ways are there of undertaking the task?
What decisions do we need to take?
How can we best use our resources?
What are the critical pathways we may need to follow?

What is desirable?

What can be done in the circumstances?

How successful can we be?

Resource needs

Have we got sufficient people?
Do we need any additional skills/expertise?
Do we need any additional kit, space, money?
How do we get any additional resources?

Individual needs

How do we recognize and use our individual contributions?
What rewards do I need?
Can I adjust my other workloads to give more commitment to the team?

Team needs

How can we work together?
How can we communicate?
How do we set standards and motivate ourselves?

Supporting systems

How good or user friendly are they?
What is your relationship with other teams/groups within an organization?
How shall we conduct our meetings?
Do we need a leader/chair?
How frequently shall we meet and where?
What do we need to do to plan and organize our meetings?

Figure 5.1 Teams and getting started: towards a methodical approach.

ple of the village would like the barn to be used for; an estate manager could be concerned with rates of return on capital; a landscape architect might look at the building in its setting and the impact of particular uses on that; a quantity surveyor might be primarily concerned about costs and a building surveyor could be concerned about the fabric of the building and the effects of any changes of use upon its structural condition.

In raising these issues, we are not trying to stereotype professional values but to illustrate how different value sets can influence perceptions of what a task may be about. We are suggesting this to reinforce the

- What does the task mean? What do we have to do?
- What are our values in relation to it?
- Do we need clarification?
- Is the brief clear?
- What are we required to produce as an end product?
- Do we need to do any preliminary investigations to examine the nature of the task?
- What is the size of the task?
- What sort of problems are we likely to be dealing with? (See Chapter 6)
- If the problems appear to be unbounded (Chapter 6) do we need to establish some boundaries?

Figure 5.2   Defining the task.

need in multi-professional teams for open discussion about values. Without such discussion it is possible that misunderstandings will arise and some of the synergy from team working will be lost.

RESOURCES

There are always difficulties in trying to estimate resource needs at the outset (Figure 5.3). Experience might tell us that there is a high probability that things will happen which could not have been foreseen. How much allowance to make for contingencies on big projects is an area of study in itself.

- Have we got the right range of expertise?
- If not, how are we going to fill the gaps?
- Have we got sufficient people?
- Are they going to be available at the right times?
- Will we need any particular kinds of help, e.g. market research interviews? Can we afford it?
- Have we got all the equipment we need?
- Can we afford to buy/hire?
- Have we got sufficient office or other space?
- Is our budget likely to be adequate?
- If not, do we need to obtain more; if so, how?

Figure 5.3   Resources.

Some of the factors that need to be considered at the planning stage are suggested in Figure 5.4. A useful tool in planning and organizing is to produce a form of flow chart which identifies the key jobs to be done, allocates who is to do them and shows the key dates for their completion (Figure 5.5).

PLANNING AND ORGANIZATION

- What time constraints are we working within?
- Can we devise a plan or strategy to complete the task?
- How much time can we afford to spend on planning and organizing?
- How do we allocate work?
- How do we allocate other resources?
- How can we monitor the quality of our work?
- How can we control or maintain the tempo of our work?
- How do we monitor progress (or lack of it)?
- How do we check and adjust our plan/strategy accordingly?
- Are there any interim stages at which we need to report progress?
- What is the significance of the final date?
- Are there other processes we need to plan for – consultations with other bodies for example?

Figure 5.4   Planning and organizing.

Particular problems can occur when decisions which teams have taken need to be ratified or agreed by some other body or groups of bodies – for example a client, the management committee of a housing association, the Fine Arts Commission, a local authority planning committee, or even the tutor for a student group. Often the delays caused by these processes and the need to reach compromises and modify proposals can test the robustness of a team.

'GROUP THINK'

It is perhaps useful at this point to mention the possible dangers associated with 'group think'. A team may become so convinced of the correctness of its own solutions or of its own ideas that it fails to recognize that there may be other (and better) solutions or ideas. 'Suspending business' (Chapter 4) in order to review and perhaps challenge conventional wisdoms within the team can be useful. A mature team wishes to learn from its actions and invests time in reviewing its processes.

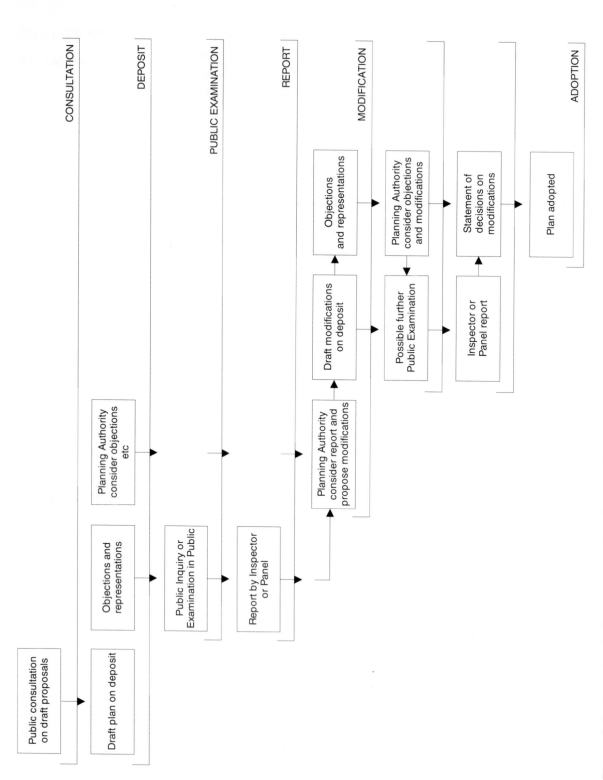

Figure 5.5 Example of a flow chart: the Development Plan preparation process.

Meetings are important to the success of all groups within the built environment. It is through meetings that groups can become teams and teams themselves become real. Teams do a great deal of their work and decision making through meetings. In this sense the effectiveness of a team may depend upon the effectiveness or otherwise of its meetings.

Team meetings may:

- act to define who is in the team and who is not – the team meeting is often the only occasion at which individuals meet each other;
- act as a means of sharing knowledge between team members – they may be about not only the immediate task but also general concerns, professional interests and social contacts;
- help to reduce the 'isolation' some members may feel – for example, those who are working in small practices at some distance away from the others;
- give an opportunity for individuals to feel that not only are their professional contributions valuable but also their general contributions to the work of the team are useful and important;
- help to generate or regenerate enthusiasm for the task that the team is undertaking;
- help to generate commitment to what the team is trying to achieve and to the decisions that the team makes.

Whether these things happen or not will depend very much on whether the meetings themselves are managed in an appropriate way.

The first decision, usually for the chair and secretary, is to decide whether or not a meeting is necessary. This may involve consultation with other members of the team. If there is insufficient business a meeting may not be necessary. Unnecessary meetings can and often do interfere with working time. Let us suppose a meeting is considered necessary.

Normally the overall planning for meetings is the responsibility of the chair/leader together with the secretary. Other participants may also need to plan ahead for a meeting – for example, by preparing progress reports or forming a view on decisions which need to be taken.

PLANNING AND ORGANIZING FOR MEETINGS

Most often a team will determine its normal pattern of meetings at an early stage in its formation. Usually such meetings are held on a weekly, fortnightly or monthly basis depending on the nature of the task. This pattern may vary throughout the life of task. There may, for example, be

FREQUENCY, TIMING AND PLACE OF MEETINGS

a need to hold more frequent meetings at the outset when there are many decisions to be made. Less frequent meetings might be necessary during the middle part when the team is working on the task in hand.

The time of day that meetings are called may be determined by many factors – availability of participants, distances to be travelled, availability of a suitable room – but we know that meetings early on Monday mornings and late on Friday afternoons tend not to be popular! Meetings held immediately after lunchtime tend to be slow.

Where to meet may be an issue for some teams. Shall we meet in London, Exeter, Birmingham or Edinburgh? Travelling distance can be a problem for some team members and can add significantly to the cost of meetings, bringing pressures to reduce their frequency and duration. Two hours should be sufficient time for most team meetings. Meetings which are anticipated to go on longer than that may have to be structured very carefully. People may become irritated or even hostile to the meeting if it is taking a long time because of inefficiency. If they expected the meeting to take two hours, then they may have arranged to do other things and will possibly have to leave.

ROOM ARRANGEMENTS   Ideally rooms for meetings should be purpose designed, and much has been written about the psychology of seating arrangements. Reality often means that we have to make do with something less than ideal but we can usually do something about the way the room is arranged. For the less formal kinds of meeting which we are concerned with, there are perhaps four golden rules:

- Everyone should be able to see and hear the Chair.
- The Chair should be able to see and hear the participants.
- Everyone should be able to see any visual material – slides, flip charts etc.
- Everyone should be reasonably comfortable and have a surface for their papers.

The room itself should be free from excessive distractions – noise, people walking through, telephones ringing, etc. Most importantly the room should be arranged to encourage 'teaminess' and participation: a circle or square arrangement is possibly best. Do not just take the room as you find it – arrange it as you want it!

Team members would normally be expected to attend every meeting. You may need to invite additional contributors, for example a structural engineer to comment upon some aspects of a design you are considering; you may need legal advice on aspects of a development. If you are to invite such contributions it is normal practice to ask them to attend for that item only and it is polite to give them a time at which the item will be discussed. Obviously you would have to structure your meeting accordingly.

Always have an agenda! Even short meetings need one. The agenda gives a guide to both the chair and the participants as to what can (and cannot) be discussed in the meeting. The agenda is also important in that it forms the basis of any notes of the meeting and any follow-through action required.

Most agendas for normal team meetings would include standard items:

- Record of apologies for absence.
- Agreeing minutes/notes of the previous meeting.
- Matters arising from the minutes not elsewhere on the agenda.
- Main business of the meeting.
- Any other business.
- Time, date and place of next meeting.

The order of items for the main business of the meeting can be important. You might consider some of the following:

- Is there a rationale to be followed – do you need information from one item before you can proceed to the next?
- Are some items likely to be contentious or difficult? Normally such items would not be dealt with right at the beginning of the agenda. You may wish the meeting to settle down before dealing with such items.
- Do some members have other commitments or have they been specially invited? Obviously if it is known that certain participants may be late or have to leave early, then items which they need to contribute to will have to be placed accordingly.

In constructing the agenda it can be useful to indicate the approximate time for discussion on each item (Figure 5.6). This also helps as a check to ensure that the agenda is not overloaded and that the meeting can be completed within the allotted time.

You may also wish to consult with team members prior to setting the agenda to see if they have particular items of business that they would like to discuss. It may also be useful to identify individuals who would take the lead on particular items. It would be normal practice to warn them in advance.

Another useful approach is to identify the action required from an item, as shown in Figure 5.6. This helps to give participants a guide to what might be required from them. It also helps them in their preparation for the meeting.

3.	Matters arising	
	(a) Meeting with T. Cramp & Son (Chair to report)	– 5 minutes
	(b) Report from NRA (M. Waterhouse to report)	– 5 minutes
4.	Barn – External painting scheme. Recommendation required (T. Muir to report)	– 20 minutes
5.	Car Park layout. For discussion (M. Waterhouse to introduce)	– 15 minutes
6.	Heritage Grant – conditions for discussion	– 10 minutes

Figure 5.6 Example of agenda items, indicating action required.

CIRCULATION OF AGENDAS Normal practice is to circulate agendas in advance of a meeting to all prospective participants. If meetings are being held very frequently this may not be possible or practicable. If the agenda is to be tabled, it is usual to allow participants to have some discussion on the coverage and ordering of the agenda. If team members are to be asked to discuss papers or reports, then ideally they should see these before the meeting. Too many papers 'tabled' at a meeting make it difficult for members to contribute effectively. This is particularly true if the information requires digestion or discussion prior to the meeting.

MINUTES AND FOLLOW-THROUGH

Let us assume that the person acting as secretary has taken notes of the meeting. These will need to be written up into minutes as soon as possible after the meeting (Figure 5.7). Early circulation of the minutes helps to get things done.

Meeting of the Much Haddock Barn Action Team
Held on 20 March 1994 at the Lamb and Flag, Much Haddock

Present: T. Collier (Chair)
             J. Bacon (Hon. Secretary)
             G. Crook
             T. Muir
             B. Rance
             M. Waterhouse

In attendance:
             D. Burns (Consultant) – Item 3 only

1. *Apologies*: D. Cassidy, D. Edden

                                   Action

2. *Minutes of previous meeting*
    The chair stated that the cost of lunch was £8.50 each not £85 each as recorded. 'Exasperated' line 3 page 2 was amended to read 'enthusiastic'. The minutes were agreed as a true record.

3. *Matters arising*
    (a) D. Burns reported that he had had a meeting with T. Cramp and Sons and they would speed up the design of the new barn.
    (b) M. Waterhouse tabled the report from the NRA which he had received that morning. Members agreed to discuss it at the next meeting.   **TEAM**

4. *Barn – External Painting Scheme*
    Members considered the three options put forward by T. Muir. After considerable discussion they agreed to recommend Option C to the District Council Planning Committee.   **CHAIR**

5. *Car Park Layout*
    M. Waterhouse explained the difficulties of access onto the B47 and would arrange a meeting with officers of the District Council.   **MW**

6. *Heritage Grant*
    The Secretary drew members' attention to the conditions attached to the award of the grant. After discussion they requested the Secretary to obtain further clarification of conditions 3a, 4e and 5d.   **SEC**

7. *A.O.B.*
    The chair reported that the Much Haddock WI Coffee morning had raised £35.20 towards the restoration fund. He had written to thank them.

8. *Date of next meeting:* 10.00 a.m. 27 March, Lamb and Flag, Much Haddock.

Figure 5.7   Example of action minutes: Much Haddock.

WHAT SHOULD BE IN THE MINUTES?

The example in Figure 5.7 indicates the normal format of action minutes. You will see that they begin with the title of the meeting, the date on which it was held and the place. The people present are recorded (i.e. the team members or group members). Others present who are not team members are listed as being in attendance. It is also normal practice to record apologies given for absence. Members who do not send apologies are not normally named.

The minutes of the previous meeting is normally a very short item which should include any amendments of fact or spelling before they are agreed. 'Matters arising' should always have a separate heading and if there is more than one they should be itemized with separate subheadings.

Discussions on agenda items are normally recorded under the same headings as the agenda. The record, which should be as brief as possible, should normally be written in reported speech. This means using the past tense; for example, 'the meeting agrees that' becomes 'the meeting agreed that'. Another convention is that officers are usually referred to by their position ('The Chair said' rather than 'Nancy Wicket said'). The record should stick to reporting the facts and try to avoid any distortion of them.

It is critically important that the minutes should record any actions to be taken by the team. For example the team 'noted' a communication from the Keep Britain Tidy Group; the team agreed to 'recommend' the adoption of Option C; B. Rance 'agreed' to produce a report for the next meeting. It can be useful to have an action column on the right-hand side of the minutes.

SUMMARY

The examples given at the beginning of the chapter indicate what might happen to two teams trying to begin a task. The examples illustrate some of the difficulties that might arise when a team has no clear purpose in its approach. The model we suggest builds on Adair's three circles of team needs and tries to indicate six areas of activity which teams might consider: defining the task; planning and organizing; identifying resource needs; needs of individuals; needs of teams; and team meetings. We suggest that consideration of these areas will help a team to make efficient progress through its early stages of development.

In addition to these six areas, teams need to give consideration to their supporting systems. We suggest good practice in relation to the way in which meetings are conducted and followed through.

CHECKLIST OF POINTS

● What difficulties might a team expect in getting started?
● What issues might a team consider in:
  – planning and organizing itself?

- – defining the task?
- – considering its resources?
- – considering both individual and team needs?
- What items might a Chair consider in the initial planning of a meeting?
- How would you construct an agenda?
- What would you take into account in selecting a room for team meetings?

REFERENCE

1. Department of the Environment (1991) *Development Plans*.

FURTHER READING

Adair, J. (1986) *Effective Team Building*, Gower.
Hirschonn, L. (1991) *Managing in the New Team Environment*, Addison-Wesley, Reading, Mass.
Janner, G. (1986) *Janner on Meetings*, Gower.
Larson, C. and La Fasto, F. (1989) *Teamwork*, Sage.
Moxon, P. (1993) *Building Better Teams*, Gower.
Seymour-Smith, L. (1984 *Making Your Meetings More Effective*, Management Update Ltd.
Tropman, J.E. (1981) *Effective Meetings*, 2nd edn, Sage.
Video Arts (1984) *More Bloody Meetings*.

CHAPTER SIX

PROBLEM SOLVING AND DECISION MAKING

GEOFF CROOK AND MIKE WATERHOUSE

THEME

Fortunately, many of the problems we face are well defined and tend to be repetitive and decisions about them can be taken in a repetitive manner.

There are circumstances, however, where decision making is beset by uncertainty and ambiguity. It is in the nature of many problems in the built environment for boundaries to be fuzzy, for the context to be messy. In the relationships between professionals and clients, public sector providers and consumers, there are boundaries that are extremely difficult for the decision maker to define. The questions often become: 'Whose problems?', 'Whose solutions?' and 'Whose values?'

OBJECTIVES

After reading this chapter you should be able to:

● examine approaches to decision making and problem solving;

● explore a staged model of decision making;

● explore the nature of problems;

● examine the process of defining objectives, generating and evaluating options;

- examine ways of making decisions in teams;

- discuss leadership and commitment to decisions.

INTRODUCTION

Decisions are an attempt to predict the future and thus can never be taken without risk. Decision making is particularly difficult where it involves different values, the weighing of unlike attributes and assessing uncertainties. Taking up the themes of Chapters 4 and 5, this chapter examines the processes of problem solving and decision making in teams.

PROBLEM SOLVING AND DECISION MAKING

Problem solving is sometimes seen as removing something that is not wanted or as finding a fault and putting it right. In its broader sense, however, it also includes the proactive seeking out and exploiting of opportunities. In this sense it requires the skills of the innovator and the entrepreneur.

Many authors use the terms 'problem solving' and 'decision making' interchangeably, as if they were the same activities. In this book they are seen as different but closely related activities. Decision making is about making choices – selecting a course of action from alternatives. Problem solving is the process of creating those alternatives. Figure 6.1 illustrates how problem solving and decision making are related.

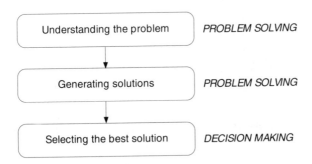

Figure 6.1 Stages of activity in problem solving and decision making.

It may be helpful to visualize the process in this way and to plan and organize actions into distinct stages of activity. These three stages

– understanding the problem, generating solutions and selecting the best solution – mainly involve analysis, design and evaluation. There can be considerable movement and overlapping between these stages and they are not always separate steps followed in a strict logical sequence. For example, by exploring possible solutions it may become apparent that there is a need to go back and re-examine the initial understanding of the problem.

Figure 6.2 illustrates another helpful way of looking at the process. A cyclical pattern of activity is shown with phases of exploration and searching followed by phases of focusing and selecting.

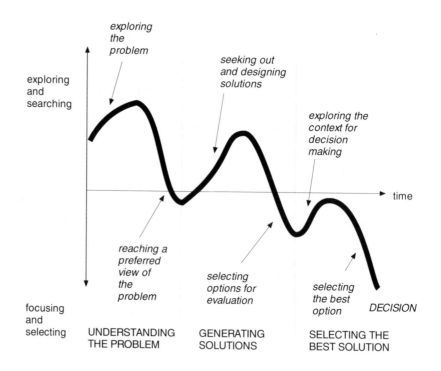

Figure 6.2   The cycle of 'exploring and searching' and 'focusing and selecting'.

The first stage of activity shown in Figure 6.2 is about understanding and describing the problem. Initially there is a searching for explanations and for different ways to look at the problem. These ideas and explanations are then narrowed down to a preferred view of the problem. The second stage, generating alternatives, begins by seeking out or designing solutions. The most desirable or promising of these are then selected to go forward to the third stage, evaluation and decision making, which also begins with an exploratory phase as the nature and the context for the decision is explored and concludes with selecting the best solution.

Problem solving and learning are closely related. Both are processes of discovery. It should be no surprise, therefore, that the strategies suggested in Chapter 2 for becoming a strategic learner could be useful in improving our ability to solve problems.

PROBLEM SOLVING SKILLS

Think of any problem you have solved recently.

- How did you solve it?
- What helped you to solve it?
- Did previous experience help?
- Do you think mental skills played a part?

Try to list the mental skills and experience which helped you solve this problem.

Do not read further until you have completed this task.

According to Adair[1], 'problem solving . . . (and decision making) . . . involve integrating previous experience and knowledge together with natural mental skills in an attempt to resolve a situation whose outcome is unknown'. Some of the mental skills and experience which contribute to successful problem solving are shown in Figure 6.3.

These ideas are supported by Kaufmann[2], who found that 'in addition to the efficient use of general problem solving strategies, it seems that expertise in problem solving is highly dependent on the availability of extensive well organised domain specific knowledge'.

Experience factors	Mental skills
Age	Memory
Previous professional/technical background	Analytical ability Logic and reasoning
Familiarity with solution-finding strategies	Synthesizing ability
Familiarity with problem content and context	Valuing ability Holistic thinking Imagination Intuition, flair Numeracy, literacy

Figure 6.3 Experience and skills for problem solving (adapted from Adair, *Creative problem solving*).

In Chapter 2 we argued that individuals approach problems in different ways depending on their preferred learning styles. We are also arguing that individuals will have strengths and weakness in specific problem-solving skills and that these will influence their approach to problem solving. If a team was being put together to solve problems it would make sense to look for a balance in learning styles, mental skills and specific knowledge. For example, if you need to form a team to investigate cost-effective solutions to provide low-cost housing in, say, Mongolia, you might look for a team with a mix of experience of similar situations and local conditions, together with people with strong imaginative and creative abilities.

UNDERSTANDING PROBLEMS
WHAT SORT OF PROBLEM IS IT?

Problems can take a variety of different forms. Francis[3] identifies several categories which can be helpful in describing a problem: puzzles, obstacles, mysteries and difficulties.

Many problems take the form of **puzzles.** If all the pieces are there, all that needs to be done is to put them back together. With a puzzle there is a 'correct' solution, or a finite number of correct solutions.

WORKPIECE 6.2

WHAT SORT OF PROBLEM IS IT?

Consider the following problems and decide what type each one is:

- Whether to become an architect or a demolition contractor.
- The barn at Much Haddock has blown down in a gale: how do you put all the pieces back together?
- Where precisely was the lost city of Atlantis?
- Your team was to give a presentation today to an important client. All the team members reported sick and there is no one else available who can do it.

- You have been asked to survey the condition of the Eiffel Tower. You suffer from vertigo.
- You would like the meadows at Much Haddock to be flower meadows. Parts of the field are contaminated by old chemical drums.

Do not read any further until you have done this workpiece.

Some problems are **obstacles** which block the way to achieving an objective; they lie in the way of where we want to go. If the blockage can be seen it may be possible to remove it, or find a way around it. Where the obstacle cannot be seen, the nature of the problem changes: it becomes a **mystery.** A problem is a mystery when something is known to be wrong, or blocking the way ahead, but the cause as yet remains unknown.

There are circumstances where the blockage is in clear view and is well understood but it is still not possible to resolve the problem. In these circumstances we are said to have a **difficulty**. There are 'subjective difficulties', where the blockage lies within ourselves – such as an inability to manage or cope with the problem. There are also 'objective difficulties', where the problem lies outside ourselves. An example would be where we have insufficient staff or equipment to deal with a problem.

Much of the work in the field of construction and development is carried out in the form of an assignment or project. An assignment or project is a contract between two parties. One party, a client or customer, specifies what is wanted. The other party agrees to do it or provide it. The key point about an assignment is that those who undertake it are not the originators of the problem or the task.

WHO SPECIFIES THE PROBLEM?

Contractors, consultants and students all carry out assignments, where they agree to carry out work which has been specified by someone else. Dealing with an assignment brings, for both parties, wide scope for ambiguity over what has been done and what needs to be done in terms of contractual arrangements. Good communication and record keeping are vital if the relationship is to work.

With an assignment it is essential that the contract is:

- understood;
- explicit;
- achievable;
- agreed.

If you are a student, test out these conditions on the next assignment you receive.

WORKPIECE 6.3

AN ASSIGNMENT

For your next assignment as a student, check the 'contract conditions':

- Is the brief clear? (For example, do I need any further information about the task?)
- Does the brief explain the criteria by which my work will be judged?

- Are the requirements of the brief realistic? (For example, can I complete the assignment in the time allowed?)
- Am I sure that my understanding of the brief is the same as that of my tutor?
- Is the brief understood, explicit and achievable? (And, if not, should I object to it?)

The sets of questions in Figures 6.4 and 6.5 are useful starting points in understanding and describing a problem or task.

How many ways are there of looking at the problem?
These could be:

spatial	–	*looking from a different direction*
or personal	–	*looking from someone else's point of view*

What do I know/need to know about this problem?
Take stock of what you know. Identify areas where further information is needed.

What am I trying to do?
Try and express this as a goal (where you want to get to, what you are trying to achieve). Begin with 'I am trying to ... '

Figure 6.4   Understanding the problem.

What are the most important issues involved?
Try to list the main factors in order of their importance.

What is the problem?
Write a simple statement that describes the crux of the problem.

How will I know when I have solved the problem?
Try to identify the criteria for success.

Figure 6.5   Describing the problem.

Some problems are well defined and the method of approaching them is clearly structured. For example, a heating and ventilation system is designed and installed. The system works well for a while but then breaks down. A skilled technical engineer diagnoses the fault and repairs the system. Solving such problems is often a routine matter of finding the fault and putting it right; of restoring the system by returning all the parts to the condition and specification implied by the original design solution.

In the above example it could be said that the solution was already known; in a sense it already existed within the original design. In solving problems of this kind it may be sufficient to apply or adapt problem-solving techniques which have been successfully used before. These techniques are likely to be logical and analytical. They could be set out as rules and procedures, as in a fault-finding manual, or involve mathematical or analogue models to predict and test out possible solutions.

This does not mean that all such problems are necessarily simple; they may involve analysing a large number of variables and making choices from a multitude of alternatives. However, known and tested techniques can be applied or adapted because the general nature of the solutions is already understood. Similar solutions have previously been found to similar problems.

Sometimes the cause of a problem may prove to be complex and deep rooted and the search for explanation reveals layer upon layer of cause–effect relationships.

One way of approaching such problems is to look for further information and to search backwards in the sequence of events to identify the cause of the cause – the problem behind the problem. This search may involve breaking down each cause and its effects into sub-parts for further detailed investigation. This analytical approach to problem solving can be highly successful and has its basis in the scientific method. Cause–effect relationships can be mapped out on 'fishbone' diagrams, a useful method in identifying specific solutions to sub-parts of a problem.

There are several limitations to such an approach to problem solving. The first (Figure 6.6) is simply that the search for the root causes which underlie the problem may never be complete. There are problems which seem to unravel into a never-ending complexity and for which investigation and analysis continue to identify more questions than explanations. Where the search for understanding appears to demand limitless information, the problem is said to be **unbounded.**

WELL-STRUCTURED PROBLEMS

MULTIPLE CAUSES: THE PROBLEM BEHIND THE PROBLEM

UNBOUNDED PROBLEMS

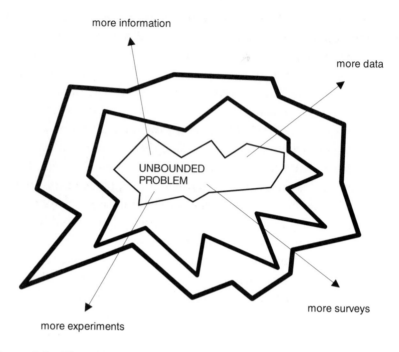

Figure 6.6 The unbounded problem.

Take, for example, a shopping centre which has been subjected to vandalism. Initial investigation suggests that the problem is related to:

● the design, in that the layout leaves hidden, enclosed areas which are not overlooked;
● the lack of effective police presence;
● the fear of local shopkeepers who say they no longer feel safe in challenging the young children they see vandalizing property;
● the more general problem of juvenile crime in this area which is itself associated with solvent and drug abuse, high youth unemployment in this area, etc.

However, unemployment might be related to other factors, and so on. We can see from this example how the area of investigation could rapidly expand as each layer of the problem is peeled off, revealing possible further causes beneath.

AMBIGUITY   People interpret the same circumstances and events in different ways, placing quite different constructions upon what they see. For example, one person may see a proposal for a new industrial development as being of vital importance, providing a source of new jobs and a welcome sign of confidence in the local economy. A second might view the proposal as the last straw in a series of unwanted developments which have ruined the local environment and destroyed the last vestiges of the community and which they see as threatening to their whole way of life. A third person, who is equally aware of the proposal, finds in it nothing of interest or of consequence.

Radically different conceptions of a problem, or of the impacts of solutions, are quite possible and therefore ambiguity can become the most difficult aspect of problem solving. In the built environment the sense of ambiguity is made often more complex by debates about who is responsible for the creation or solution of a problem.

WORKPIECE 6.4

CARDBOARD CITY

Consider the plight of people sleeping rough in a 'cardboard' city.

● Who might feel that they are a problem?

● Who might be affected by rough sleepers in such a cardboard city?
● Who might be responsible for resolving this problem?

NEW IDEAS AND HYPOTHESES

Most of the analytical techniques used in problem solving are concerned with reducing complexity. Approaches centred on creative thinking are particularly useful where a problem is novel and ill defined. An important part of such a task is to formulate or reformulate the problem itself.

A further limitation of the analytical approach to problem solving is that in analysing data we tend to use very simple conceptual frameworks such as 'correlation' or 'cause and effect'. De Bono[4] argues that we have a very limited repertoire of such hypotheses and, as illustrated in Figure 6.7, that analysing data can do little more than provide evidence to support or reject them.

What analysis alone can never do is produce radically new ideas, concepts or new ways of looking at the world. De Bono's position is that: '. . . the tradition of problem solving and removal of causes are valid as far as they go but they are only part of the thinking required . . . they exclude opportunity thinking, initiative thinking, enterprise, improvement, and all those types of thinking in which we set out to think about things which are not wrong.'

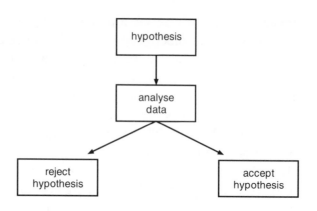

Figure 6.7 Hypothesis testing.

GENERATING SOLUTIONS INNOVATION AND CREATIVITY IN PROBLEM SOLVING

The generation of new solutions is often constrained by preconceived ideas about what sort of solutions are feasible and where they might be found. There is a tendency to look for solutions in areas where they have been found before. It is difficult to break with old habits and to explore new ways of thinking. In the search for new ideas in problem solving, it can be helpful to suspend judgement as to what might normally be considered rational and reasonable and to allow the search to go in new directions. Nolan[5] stresses the importance of being able to approach a problem with a mix of two kinds of mindset: the reasonable and the unreasonable, the rational and the non-rational. For him the key is: '. . . to recognise when each is appropriate and to move easily and comfortably between the two. To get locked into the logical analytical end of the spectrum is to cut yourself off from your ability to invent and innovate. To be a successful problem solver you need to approach each problem with the right state of mind.'

There is a wealth of literature on this subject and Vincent Nolan's *Innovator's Handbook* is a useful starting point for those who wish to experiment with creative techniques. Some examples of these techniques are discussed below.

BRAINSTORMING   Brainstorming is a means of generating large numbers of ideas. The technique involves deferring judgement. It can be practised by an individual but is more commonly used as a group technique. Individuals are asked to suggest ideas and criticism is forbidden, no matter how strange or infeasible an idea might appear. The approach is to strive for quantity rather quality. The principle behind brainstorming is that the more ideas you have, the better is the chance of finding a good one.

There are two general difficulties in effective brainstorming and it may take practice to appreciate the value of this technique. One is that it can be hard to resist making instant judgements and to screen out many ideas as soon as they appear. The second is that even when ideas have been generated it is easy to dismiss everything that is new or untried as impracticable or unacceptable. If brainstorming is to contribute to the search for new solutions it is important to explore the potential of each idea and to look for new insights and new connections.

THE IDEAL SOLUTION This is also a method in which constraints are relaxed but there is time to allow the design of one ideal solution. Whilst this solution should be operationally viable (it should work), the method encourages creativity and the exploration of ideas previously precluded. Idealized design is useful in 'breaking the mould' of our thinking, particularly where we are stuck in a 'get rid of what we do not like' style of problem solving. Ackoff[6] describes such negative approaches as 'walking into the future facing the past – we move away from, rather than towards something'. Designing idealized solutions allows us to face the future and specify where we want to go. There is always a chance that we might find a way of reaching the ideal solution, or of arriving somewhere close by. At the very least, by envisaging how we want the future to be, we can help to make our objectives and values explicit.

WORKPIECE 6.5

IDEALIZED DESIGN

Think about any swimming pool you have been to. Imagine you are there now.

● Write a list of those things you dislike about it and would like put right.

Try to visualize your ideal swimming pool.

● Write a list of those features which you find attractive in this idealized design.

A comparison of these two lists should demonstrate the creative advantage of looking forward to an ideal solution rather than fault finding and putting things right.

WORKING BACKWARDS AND FORWARDS This is an extension of the 'ideal solution' method. By reversing the more usual approach and working backwards from an ideal solution, it may be possible to find 'stepping stones' or 'staging points' back towards 'where we are now'.

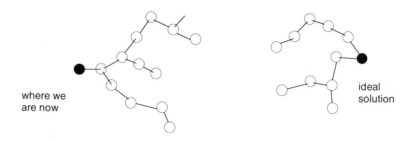

where we
are now

ideal
solution

Figure 6.8   Working backwards and forwards (based on De Bono[4]).

Figure 6.8 illustrates how it is possible to experiment with paths to an idealized solution by working backwards and exploring routes forward simultaneously. Again, even if the ideal solution proves to be unattainable, this method encourages positive thinking, the releasing of ideas and the challenging of existing boundaries and routes.

SIEVING AGAINST CONSTRAINTS   There can be circumstances in which there is an embarrassment of potential solutions and the problem becomes how to reduce their number and select the best alternatives for evaluation. If there was, say, a glut of office space on the market and we were looking to rent, an approach could be to sieve out the infeasible or the less desirable options by identifying criteria. Some criteria might be identified as absolute constraints – factors which were seen as essential parts of any solution. Others could be selection criteria – factors which reflect strong preferences.

In Figure 6.9 five constraints are shown set out horizontally along the top of a grid, with the options listed vertically. Each option is assessed in turn and where it hits one or more constraints it is rejected as infeasible.

If the constraints were spatial (say, a drainage catchment or a green belt), it might be easier to eliminate options by plotting a constraints map. The mapping and sieving of large numbers of spatial factors has been made more practicable with the introduction of computer aided tools such as geographic information systems (GISs). The general disadvantage of such methods is that they exclude custom designed solutions.

Constraints

	1	2	3	4	5	
OPTION A		✗			✗	reject
OPTION B				✗		reject
OPTION C						accept for evaluation
OPTION D	✗		✗			reject

further options

Figure 6.9 The constraints sieve.

STRATEGIES: OPTIMIZING, 'SATISFICING' AND DIS-SOLVING A solution to a problem can only be as good as the ideas and the options generated. But how good does a solution have to be? Is it necessary or desirable to seek out the best solution? It would have to be the best with a 'puzzle', as there are only correct solutions. For example, if you were reassembling a structure and found that the last strut was too long, would it be acceptable as a solution to cut a piece from one end to make it fit?

In some circumstances it could be that the first feasible solution that appears would be acceptable. This approach is called **satisficing**. Suppose, for example, that a party of climbers was exposed on a mountainside, in need of protection from wind and rain. It would be unwise of them to delay the building of an emergency shelter until they could be sure that they had designed the most elegant or aesthetically pleasing solution. The first feasible viable solution would surely do. There are strategies, therefore, to be considered in generating solutions. **Optimizing** – seeking the best solution – may be the ideal strategy, but this has to be weighed against factors such as time and cost.

There are situations in which, despite all the best creative ability, experience and effort, a solution cannot be found. Some problems are insoluble. If it is accepted that no solution exists, or that it cannot be found, then one option sometimes available is to **dissolve the problem**. This involves modifying the problem definition, which might be possible where the criteria or constraints to a problem are internal; that is, within your control. An example would be where you wanted to buy a four-bedroom house within a 30-minute commuting time of your place of work. After six months of intensive searching you finally accept that such properties exist, but they are beyond your financial means. As you are sick of living in rented accommodation you dissolve the problem by considering three-bedroom houses or properties beyond a 30-minute commuting time. In this case it has been accepted that the original problem could not be solved; the problem has been reframed.

DECISION MAKING

Decision making is about making choices, selecting a course of action from alternatives. The purpose of decision making is to make the best possible choice of action. However, the best choice of action is not necessarily the same as the best solution to the problem. For example, it has already been said that the ideal solution may be unattainable, or too costly, or too long in the design. Decisions inevitably involve making judgements, weighing advantages and disadvantages and balancing risks against potential gains.

HOW IS THE DECISION GOING TO BE MADE?

Managers rarely have complete discretion in decision making; they act as agents for others. It is therefore important to clarify the constraints and boundaries to a decision. Is anyone else involved in making the decision? Who should be consulted? Faced with any decision it is important to clarify 'why' and 'how' the decision is to be made. What is intended by the decision? What is the desired outcome? On what basis is evaluation to be carried out? The list of questions in Figure 6.10 may be a useful starting point.

There is no one best starting point or ideal sequence for decision making: in the end the route actually taken is likely to be cyclical and iterative, revisiting some stages.

DECISION MAKING IN TEAMS

Mature teams which have reached the 'flexible' or the 'performing' stages of development (Chapter 4) will have well developed processes for taking decisions. Such teams are likely to have explored, perhaps through trial and error, a number of different ways of arriving at decisions and will have finally reached a mutual understanding and a commitment to an approach which works effectively for them.

For newly formed groups, faced with their first tasks, the need to sort out a process for decision making is not always seen as a priority. Filled with enthusiasm and keen to get on and make progress with the task, it is not surprising that it is usually the task, rather than processes for achieving the task, that initially commands the attention of a new

- Why is there a need to make a decision?

- Who is involved in making the decision?

- What are the goals, objectives or targets that have to be achieved?

- How important is the decision?

- Does the decision need to be made quickly, or could it be delayed?

- Is the decision irrevocable, or could it be changed if it all goes wrong?'

- What dangers and risks are involved?

- What options are available?

- How can options be generated?

- How much time and effort should be given to the search for options?

- What are the criteria for decision making?

- How will the choice between alternative courses of action be made?

- Is the decision a 'one-off' or is it dependent on other decisions being made?

- Who is involved in implementing the decision?

Figure 6.10   Making decisions.

group. The main pitfalls for new groups in making decisions are:

- a failure to use all the resources of the team in making a decision;
- a failure to achieve commitment to a decision.

LEADERS AND GROUP DECISION MAKING   It can sometimes be helpful in decision making if a group can find a member who is prepared to act as leader and who can find general support for taking on that role. Many tasks are of course dealt with by groups which have been set up within a management hierarchy and where a leader has already been vested with the authority and responsibility for leading the group and achieving the task. There are many approaches that group leaders can adopt for group decision making.

The 'continuum of leadership behaviour'[7], illustrated in Figure 6.11, can be helpful in looking at the use of authority by a group leader and at the variety of ways in which members of a group might wish to be treated. Six 'styles' of leadership are shown ranging from the autocratic 'tell' to the enabling 'facilitate'.

At one extreme of this continuum, the leader is autocratic, taking all of the decisions, and **tells** the group what is to be done. Moving along this continuum, the leader still takes all the decisions but **sells** it to the rest of the group through explanation and persuasion. With both of these styles the leader owns the problem and the task; the role of the group is simply to carry out the leader's decisions.

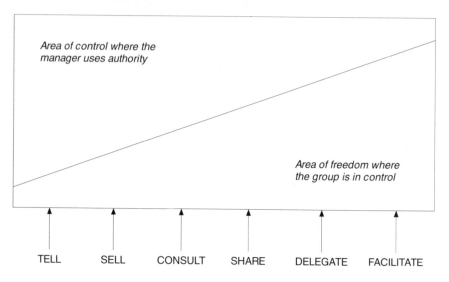

Figure 6.11   Continuum of leadership behaviour (adapted from Tannenbaum and Schmidt[7]).

In a **consultative** style the leader encourages the group to bring forward suggestions for achieving the task. The leader still takes all the decisions, but in doing so takes account of the ideas put forward by the other team members. With the **sharing** style of leadership the leader encourages the whole group to participate in the making of decisions. The leader may still be involved in taking the decisions and retains control over what is decided by setting limits to the discretion of other team members. An important feature of both the consultative and the sharing styles is that problems, solutions and decisions are openly discussed by the group as a whole. The leader tries to build a decision, by drawing on the experience and skills of every member of the group.

A leader adopting a **delegating** style identifies areas of the task where other members are to take decisions. The leader takes little part in the decision making and simply reserves the power to steer the overall direction of the group. At the far end of this spectrum of leadership styles is the **facilitating** leader who takes no direct part in any of the decisions about the task. The facilitator enables others to take decisions by providing a supportive environment.

For a leader appointed by the group the leadership style ultimately adopted is likely to be influenced by three factors: the natural leadership style of the leader; the ability of the leader to adopt different leadership styles; and how the members of the team want to be led, or are prepared to be led.

In relation to the last of these factors it may be helpful to consider the continuum of leadership behaviour again, looking at it this time from the point of view of the individual members of the group. As part of a group working on a task, how do they want to be treated? Each person may have a different answer. Some may feel that the task and context are quite new to them and they are prepared to follow the leadership of others, who are perhaps more knowledgeable, experienced or confident in their abilities. Others who have some relevant knowledge and expertise may feel that they have much to contribute and could become frustrated if they are not allowed to participate, or at least be consulted in decisions taken about the task.

If the leader has the ability to adopt a range of management styles, one approach could be to treat individuals differently according to their preferences and their needs. Adopting a mixed leadership style can however create difficulties if the signals between the leader and individual members of the group become misdirected, confused and unclear. Consistency in leadership style is important. It takes time for a group to learn to work together and develop the skills of a team. The mutual understandings and relationships, hard won by a group in their pursuit of team skills, can easily be damaged by a leader who tries to change style too quickly.

Where leaders have been given the role and responsibility for group leadership within the context of an organization, there are many other issues which impinge upon leadership style. It is likely, for example, that the organization will itself have a distinctive style of management. Many organizations, through policy and training, encourage their employees to adopt a particular approach. The culture and style of companies and how they may choose to manage change is a subject of topical interest in management literature.

One of the most common reasons for a group's dissatisfaction with their first appointment of a leader, however, is that their method of taking this decision was itself flawed, often for the reasons given above.

COMMITMENT TO DECISIONS

One problem often faced by groups that have not yet reached the skilled stage of an effectively performing team is that, whilst they may be able to reach decisions, they have difficulty in achieving commitment to the decisions they have made. For the newly formed group this can be the source of great frustrations and conflict. Individuals may spend time on work that they thought had been planned and agreed, only to find subsequently that there has been a 'false consensus' and that this was not so.

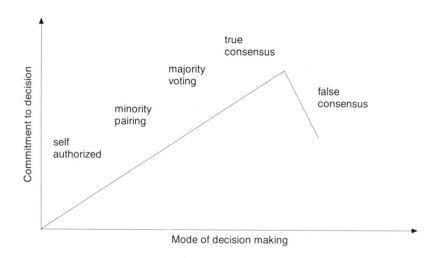

Figure 6.12 Commitment to decision making (adapted from Adair[1]).

Figure 6.12 illustrates that some modes of decision making attract higher levels of commitment than others. Consider the following:

> Example:
> 'Everyone agree?' asks the person chairing the meeting.
>
> No one replies.
>
> 'Well, I'll take it that silence means agreement. The next item on the agenda is . . .'

In this example of a decision being made, no one except the people sitting around the table is likely to know whether there really was agreement or not. The notes of the meeting simply record that there was agreement to a decision; but now they are all committed, although many may not have agreed with the decision at all.

One of the features of belonging to a group (team or committee) is that once a decision is taken by a group, then all the members must abide by it, even though individuals may have had their dissension recorded or may have lost in a vote. In making decisions in meetings, it is important to recognize that individuals who are party to a decision may feel quite different degrees of commitment to it.

Figure 6.12 illustrates how the degree of commitment to decision making can be influenced by the method by which decisions are taken. There are several ways by which groups of people can arrive at decisions and we shall now consider them.

POWER OR SELF-AUTHORIZATION Here the most powerful person in terms of, say, status, seniority or personality puts forward an idea or manipulatively supports that of another member. This idea is then pursued until it has the support of the whole group. The level of commitment to decisions taken in this way tends to be low.

> Example:
> A forceful chair states: 'I believe that we should follow the course of action set out in my report. Everyone agreed? Good.'

More cunningly, perhaps, the chair waits for another to refer to an idea.

> Example:
> 'I believe that Tom's suggestion, that we should now go forward with Option B, is the right course of action. Anybody disagree?'

Tom, perhaps naively, had simply raised the possibility of Option B without necessarily suggesting that it was the best course of action. In the meeting, however, he finds it difficult to contradict the powerful chair. Most of the members of the group like Tom and if they now contradict or question the proposal it will appear that they are opposing him.

In both of these examples individuals in the group, whilst expected to take part in decision making, felt constrained in the meeting from questioning, exploring or challenging the views being put forward. There may have been much they could have usefully contributed to the building of a decision but in the event, faced with a powerful and manipulative chair, they were unable to do so. It would not be surprising if some members of the group, unhappy with how they have been treated and perhaps feeling dissatisfied with their own performance, begin to waver in their support for the decision.

MINORITY SUBGROUP OR PAIRING Here usually two of the more articulate (or organized) members of a group put forward an idea and support each other. Done with subtlety this is a very effective way for a small group within a team to influence the rest. The remainder of the group will not usually object; they will have opportunities to challenge and explore the issues but will usually meet prepared assurances from one or other of the pairing.

> Example:
> 'I'd like to support David's idea. I think it would give us just the right level of flexibility,' says Jean.
>
> 'Have we got the resources?' asks Tony.
>
> 'Yes,' says Jean, positively. 'I estimate that we would need another three staff for one week, but this would be possible if we delay the start until April.'

And so it goes on as planned, with David and Jean supporting one another and fielding questions, the replies to many of which they have had time to discuss in advance. Provided this approach does not become the norm, and the Davids and Jeans do not win every time, this may be tolerated by the rest of the group. Decisions arrived at in this way may not attract the highest commitment from all members of a group, but they tend to be more acceptable than self-authorized decisions promoted by one powerful member.

MAJORITY VOTING With this type of decision a majority of the group votes in favour of a particular course of action. What is often not disclosed is the basis on which individuals made their vote. An individual may have been influenced by considerations which bear little relation to the issues discussed when the group met to take the decision. The decision may, for example, turn upon a vote against another individual. Where this happens the strength of feeling amongst the minority, and hence their commitment to the decision, may be unknown.

Example:
'Okay,' said the chair, 'Jean's put her case for Option A and Tom has put the case for Option B. You've had the chance to hear their arguments and ask questions. As this is a difficult decision and there is clearly still some disagreement, I think the fairest way forward is to take a vote. All those in favour of . . . '

Faced with a minority there can be uncertainties about their power, or their intentions to frustrate the course of action intended by the majority.

This can therefore be a risky way of proceeding, although it does give a democratic feel to the decision making process. A further disadvantage of majority voting is that it can prevent the best option from being discussed or ever seeing the light of day.

Consensus is the best mode of decision making for reaching high levels of commitment within a team. Decision making by true consensus, however, is both difficult to recognize and difficult to achieve.

Example:
'Fine,' says the chair, 'we have had a full discussion of all the options. Am I correct in saying that you would all support Option C, as being the best course of action in the circumstances? Tom, Jean, David, Brian . . . are we all in agreement? Good, we have a decision.'

In this example the chair, acutely aware of the dangers of false consensus, specifically asks each member of the team if they were in agreement with the decision.

SUMMARY

Decision making is about making choices – selecting a course of action from alternatives. Problem solving is the process of creating those alternatives. Problem solving and decision making cover the range of activities from the reactive 'putting things right' to the more proactive 'seeking out and exploiting of opportunities'. There are three general stages of activity: understanding and describing the problem; generating alternatives; selection and decision making. Each stage tends to begin with a phase of exploration and searching followed by a phase of focusing and selection.

Problem solving and learning are closely related. Both are processes of discovery. In Chapter 2 it was said that individuals approach problems in different ways depending on their preferred learning styles.

They will also have strengths and weaknesses in specific problem-solving skills, such as those in Adair's list. If a team was being put together to solve problems it would make sense to look for a balance in learning styles, mental skills and specific knowledge.

Problems can take a variety of different forms from puzzles, obstacles and blockages to mysteries, opportunities and assignments. Much of the work in the field of construction and development is carried out in the form of an assignment which is a contract between two parties. Those who undertake an assignment are not the originators of the task and it is essential that the contract is understood, explicit, achievable and agreed.

Some problems are well defined and the method of approaching them is clearly structured. Others prove to be complex and the cause of the problem is deep rooted, with layer upon layer of cause–effect relationships. One way of approaching such problems is to look for further information and to search backwards in the sequence of events to identify the cause of the cause – the problem behind the problem. This analytical approach to problem solving has a number of limitations. One is that the search for the root causes, which underlie the problem, may never be complete. Another is that in analysing data we tend to use very simple conceptual frameworks. Most of the analytical techniques used in problem solving are concerned with reducing complexity.

Many problems in the fields of planning, construction and development are extremely messy and include not only complexity but also novelty and ambiguity. With such problems it is often an important part of the task to formulate the problem itself. A solution to a problem can only be as good as the ideas and the options generated. Analysis on its own will not produce new concepts and ideas. Creative thinking is important in making new connections and insights and challenging accepted wisdoms.

Two of the main pitfalls for new groups in making decisions are failing to use all the resources of the team and failing to achieve commitment for their decisions. It can be helpful in decision making if a group finds a leader who can find general support for taking on that role. The 'continuum of leadership behaviour' identified by Tannenbaum and Schmidt is useful in explaining leadership styles and how individuals in a team may want to be treated.

The 'mode', or way in which decisions are made, often correlates with the commitment of team members. 'False consensus' is often a problem for the newly formed group. Members appear to support (or at least not oppose) a particular decision in a meeting but subsequently show little commitment to it.

- What experience factors and mental skills contribute to successful problem solving?
- What contractual conditions would you expect to find with an assignment?
- In what ways are 'well-structured' and 'unbounded' problems different?
- What are the limitations of analytical approaches to problem solving?
- Why might innovation and creativity be important in problem solving?
- What is meant by 'optimizing', 'satisficing' and 'dissolving' a problem?
- How might the 'mode' or way in which a decision is made by a group influence the level of commitment to a decision?
- What are the six 'styles' of leadership suggested by Tannenbaum and Schmidt's 'Continuum of Leadership Behaviour'?
- In what ways might the mode of decision making affect the level of commitment to the decisions made by a team?

REFERENCES

1. Adair, J. (1986) *Effective Team Building*, Gower.
2. Kaufmann, A. (1968) *The Science of Decision Making*. World University Library, Weidenfeld and Nicholson.
3. Francis, D. (1990) *Effective Problem Solving*, Routledge.
4. De Bono, E. (1982) *Thinking in Action*, BBC Enterprises Ltd.
5. Nolan, V. (1989) *The Innovator's Handbook*, Sphere Books Ltd.
6. Ackoff, R.L. (1978) *The Art of Problem Solving*, John Wiley & Sons Inc., New York.
7. Tannenbaum, R. and Schmidt, W.H. (1973) How to choose a leadership pattern. *Harvard Business Review*, May–June, Harvard, USA.

FURTHER READING

Henry, J. (1991) *Creative Management*, Sage Publications Ltd.
Morgan, G. (1983) *Imaginization*, Sage Publications Inc.

PART THREE

LEARNING ABOUT THE PRINCIPAL AREAS OF BUSINESS MANAGEMENT

MANAGEMENT AND ORGANIZATIONS

JOHN BRUNSDON

THEME

An organization may be defined as a group of people working together over a period of time to achieve a common goal. Most professionals do, or eventually will, perform a management role in such an organization. This chapter looks at a range of built environment organizations and provides ways of understanding their nature, the way they are structured and what is meant by organizational culture. It also discusses some of the main influences and theories which have contributed to our knowledge of organizations.

OBJECTIVES

After reading this chapter you should be able to:

● explore an organizational model;

● discuss the need for functional areas within an organization;

● describe the characteristics of flat, tall and matrix structures;

● discuss the meaning of centralization and decentralization;

● describe what is meant by organization cultures;

● discuss the main influences and theories which have contributed to our knowledge of organizations.

INTRODUCTION

We live in an organizational society and the world these organizations have created is very different from the social world 200 years ago. From this proposition it would seem that organizations are different from tribes, classes, ethnic groups or families. In other words organizations are created by humans – they are simply social units or human groupings deliberately constructed (and reconstructed) to carry out specific tasks. Organizations will vary in size from a one-person unit to the large multinational business organization employing thousands, and their tasks will cover the whole gamut of human needs and wants.

As organizations are artificial constructs they can, in theory, change their form as human needs change, or disappear altogether as people get their wants and needs satisfied in cheaper or better ways by alternative organizations. The most prolific type of organization is the small business firm – it seems that there is a very strong desire in many individuals to work for themselves. Such businesses are born and die according to their success or failure; they rarely survive the death or retirement of their original founder but some manage to transfer themselves over time into stable family-owned businesses and a few grow into mighty companies. These last are easily recognized in our society for their founders become knights, barons, etc. (Lord Nuffield started with a bicycle repair shop, Lord Leverhulme with a grocery shop selling soap, amongst others things; in more recent history Akio Morita, co-founder of Sony, the Japanese electronics empire, started with $400 and 10 men.)

We are living at a time of rapid social, economic and cultural change and our organizations are undergoing massive restructuring – voluntary or forced – to cope with new societal demands. This means new organizational structures, new professions and new methods of working together.

A MODEL

All organizations can be viewed as operating along four interrelating axes:

- **Task and objectives** – what is the organization trying to do?
- **The people** that the organization has available to carry out its objectives (these can be financially rewarded or volunteers).
- **The methods.** Our society, as a result of the activities of organizations, is very rich in the artefacts with which to produce goods and services. It is important to appreciate that the existing technology (quill pen or sophisticated computer) determines not only what goods and services can be produced but also the working methods by which those goods and services are produced.
- **The organization** – the way in which the work of human beings in organizations is arranged around the available technology to carry out the tasks and objectives. It is probably true to say that

there are more failures in business and systems from inappropriate organization structures than occur from producing the 'wrong' goods and services.

Using these four axes, which are illustrated in Figure 7.1, it is now possible to draw our first model of an organization. It could be any organization – private or public, small or large, commercial or social, from ICI or BT to the local tennis club or play-group.

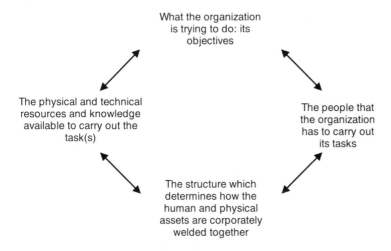

What the organization is trying to do: its objectives

The physical and technical resources and knowledge available to carry out the task(s)

The people that the organization has to carry out its tasks

The structure which determines how the human and physical assets are corporately welded together

Figure 7.1 The four interrelating axes of an organization.

These axes are interacting: a change in one will necessitate changes of varying magnitude in the other three. Historical examples involve railway and motorway construction. Between 1830 and 1848 a commercial opportunity arose in the UK to build railways (the use of iron railroads having been perfected together with an efficient steam engine in the coal-mines). The capital funds needed were available and so was a labour force (Figure 7.2).

If we now change the task to a similar kind of undertaking in the twentieth century, the model will look like Figure 7.3.

Comparing these two models it is very easy to see that, although the tasks undertaken were very similar in their main aspects (viz. a transport system), the dynamics of modern technology and a skilled labour force produced very different organizational demands. The simplified model can now be slighty amended: Figure 7.4 shows the technology axis in two

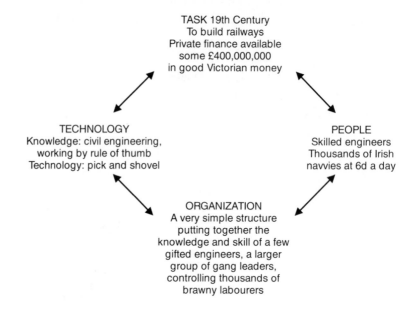

Figure 7.2   Organizational model: nineteenth century railway building.

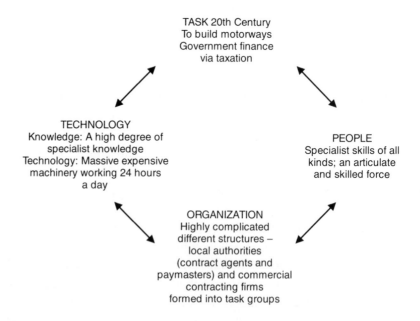

Figure 7.3   Organizational model: twentieth century motorway building.

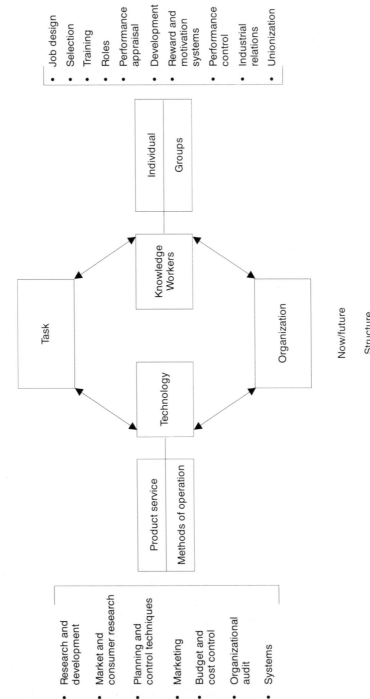

Figure 7.4 Organizational model: division of the axes.

parts to indicate that the current level of technology decides not only what goods and services can be produced, but also the ways and methods by which goods and services are produced. This leads to two main questions:

- How effective is the organization? Does it actually do what it was set up to do?
- How efficient is the organization in carrying out its tasks? In other words, does the organization make maximum use of the resources available or is there underutilization?

FUNCTIONAL MANAGEMENT AND ORGANIZATIONAL STRUCTURES

As organizations grow and change, so the need for specialists alters and organizational shapes assume different configurations.

Organizations usually have some kind of legal identity – if only for tax purposes. (This is discussed further in Chapter 8.) They therefore have a corporate life which, while constantly changing, is different from that of its members. Figure 7.5 illustrates how the shape of an organization and its internal structure depends on how it has responded to the threats and opportunities in its environment.

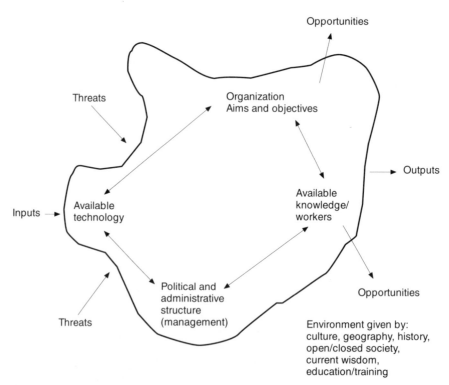

Figure 7.5 The shape of an organization dependent on reactions to threats and opportunities in the environment.

Organizations of all sizes take resources from the environment and by their operating practices convert these resources into goods and services. Some of the resources are needed to maintain the operating structure. Organizations therefore 'buy in' resources, converting a proportion of these into goods and services whilst using the remainder to 'make or do' things inside the organization. Decisions that influence this balance between 'buy in' and 'make or do' can be critical as they can affect the organization's performance.

In Figure 7.5 a shape has been drawn around the original model of Figure 7.1. Looking at the historical process of business organizational growth, it is possible to see how the organizational profile changes.

Most organizations start small, with one or two people. If the organization is successful other staff are engaged (Figure 7.6).

Figure 7.6   The small organization.

In the small organization knowledge is held by the entrepreneur or specialist and employees are divided in two groups: skilled individuals and general labour.

If the organization is successful there is growth or expansion. Figure 7.7 shows the organization expanding with supervisory levels as the foremen/supervisors extend the eyes and ears of the owner/boss.

As size increases further, parts of the boss's work are split off into functional areas and later into separate departments each with its own hierarchy of employees. Figure 7.8 illustrates an organization with functional management and departments.

As the need for more capital arises, the organization is forced to look elsewhere for finance. This is facilitated by concepts of incorporation and limited liability and is legitimized by Acts of Parliament (Chapter 8). Figure 7.9 illustrates the emergence of the manager or chief officer of functional areas.

The functional department has now arrived as well as the functional

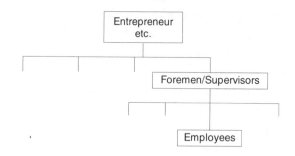

Figure 7.7   Supervisory levels within the expanding organization.

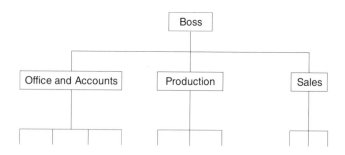

Figure 7.8   An organization with functional levels. Work is split horizontally; control is split vertically.

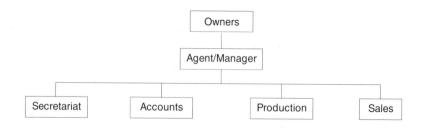

Figure 7.9   The manager of functional areas.

manager (Figure 7.10), who has come from any discipline or profession. At this stage the employees tend to be divided sharply into workers and office staff.

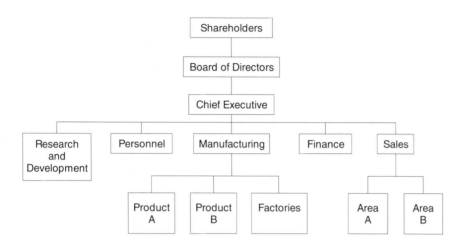

Figure 7.10   Functional manager and functional departments.

LOCAL AUTHORITY STRUCTURES

Visit your own local authority and ask for a chart which shows an outline structure of the organization as a whole. As local authorities are large organizations their activities are inevitably split into functional areas with functional managers.

Look at those areas of the organization which are likely to include activities of built environment professionals – such as planning, housing, engineering/surveying and architecture. These may be identified as specific functional areas, each with its chief officers reporting directly to a chief executive, shown as forming part of a corporate management group. Alternatively, these parts of the organization may be grouped together in some way, perhaps in a department of technical services. You may be able to show evidence in the organization chart which suggests that some parts of a service are being contracted out.

The organization, now large, has profilerated at several levels of management apart from the lower levels of control needed to produce goods and services at the workface of the organization. This produces the very tall organization shown in Figure 7.11.

Senior management

Middle management

Junior management

Workforce

Figure 7.11   Layers of management.

Size brings problem of control. The bureaucratic solution means another level of management but this tends to create problems of communication, with the remoteness of top management removed from what actually happens at the workforce level. A high degree of centralization means a large HQ staff. Senior managers normally have contracts of service; the rest of the employees are still covered by master and servant legislation but at this size the business attracts the attention of organized labour. It may be that the workforce will become unionized.

The rationale behind such traditional structures has been the measurement and control of output and performance of the workforce. Organizations structured in this way, however, tend to have difficulties in performing their tasks effectively.

We now consider two possible solutions – decentralization and/or the development of matrix structures.

A DECENTRALIZED ORGANIZATION

Organizations appear to operate along a continuum of centralization–decentralization as complexities of size and national and international operations have to be addressed. Large organizations, whether private or public, change their shape as they move along this continuum. There are periods when head office (the centre) delegates decision making and control to the operating units and divisions. At other times head office brings back control to the centre because the operating units seem to be going in different directions from the desired objectives of the organization. At present there are strong movements towards decentralization leading to small head offices with fewer levels of management and leaner operating units.

Organizations can decentralize in a number of ways. Some do so by product service group, others by area, or a combination of these (Figure 7.12).

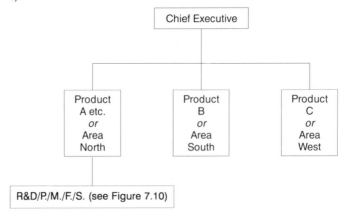

Figure 7.12 A decentralized organization – decentralization by product/service groups or by areas (local, regional, national, international).

DECENTRALIZATION IN LOCAL GOVERNMENT

Services provided by local government are increasingly being provided at a more local level. Area and neighbourhood offices and the introduction of the Local Management of Schools (LMS) are examples of this movement towards decentralization.

Choose either the education or housing service of your local authority and look for examples of decentralization. Go to a local secondary school or area housing office and collect a range of material that is provided for the information of local users of that service. Try to obtain organizational charts of the local authority as a whole and for the particular service you have chosen to study.

● Draw a chart of the organizational structure showing the relationship between the central and locally provided areas.

● Try to find examples of decisions which can be made by decentralized sub-units of the service. (For example, what decisions, if any, can be made at an area housing office? What new areas of decision making were devolved down to schools when LMS was introduced?)

● How are decentralized units of the service accountable for their actions? (Is the service managed at the local level completely free to make some decisions and/or are there mechanisms of control through which it has to report back to the centre?)

● What opportunities are there for people to gain access to, or to influence, the provision of the service at the local level?

A PROJECT ORGANIZATION

With the complexity of tasks now facing organizations in our society, specialists from several functional areas need to work together. This leads to a project organization (Figure 7.13). Specialists are in theory 'on loan' from the functional departments and work together on projects until they are completed.

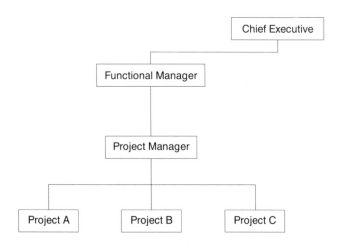

Figure 7.13 Project organization.

A MATRIX ORGANIZATION

Increasingly, because of the complexity of the tasks they are required to perform, project organizations develop into matrix configurations (Figure 7.14).

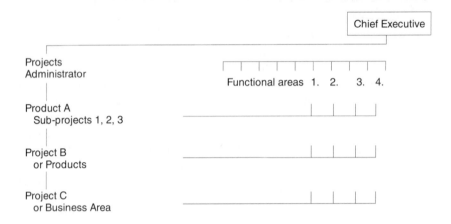

Figure 7.14   Matrix organization.

Some matrix organizations are very complex. An outstanding example is NASA, the US National Aeronautical Space Administration which first put a man on the moon and brought him back. The technological breakthrough associated with the space programme is still affecting our lives and our organizations. Advances in solid state physics and the invention of the silicon chip made space travel possible through the miniaturization of computer systems. The silicon chip has taken over our organizations, changing what goods and services can be produced and the work structures which produce these goods and services. Organizations are being re-engineered, or 'de-layered' as the process is sometimes called. Head offices are disappearing into shells, while the number of employees needed in most of our organizations is still shrinking. More and more of the specialists and professionals required by modern society are working on contract or for fees and increasingly from a home base rather than an office.

Local authorities may be moving towards structures with a small core of staff on fixed-term contracts (Figure 7.15).

THE CULTURE OF ORGANIZATIONS

The organizational chart does not, of course, give the whole picture – simply the formal structure, one axis of our model. The formal structure has to be staffed. Despite the rational job descriptions and job titles,

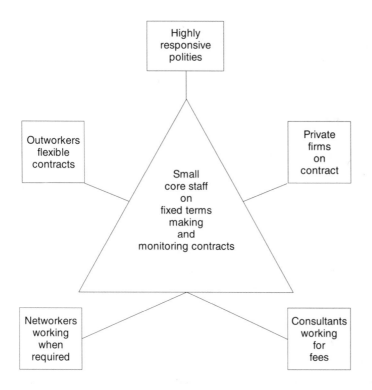

Figure 7.15 A local authority with a small core of staff.

staff will act as people. Feelings, hopes and fears, likes and dislikes, are not left behind in the outside world, beyond the organizational boundaries. This leads to groupings of like-minded and like-feeling people within the organization, who collectively make up the informal groups or networks that form the social life of the organization and permeate the whole organization – employees and management.

Taking part in this social life is often an important part of employment and withdrawal from it can add to the burden of redundancy or retirement. For the same reason, not everybody can work as a home-based networker.

The organizational chart does not explain what it is like for that particular organization as compared with another one, despite the fact that both are working in the same field.

'Culture', an idea borrowed from sociology, can be used to illuminate how organizations work:

● Their deepest beliefs about how their work should be organized.

● The way in which management authority should be exercised, people rewarded and personnel controlled.

The culture, which permeates the entire organization, can be so dominant as to describe (for example) how employees should dress and where senior staff are expected to live.

The 'culture' approach was first developed by Roger Harrison, an American engineer, in an attempt to explain why the American system of doing things was less successful when applied in another country and another culture. While American business value systems could be reasonably transferred to American companies operating in the UK, there were decided difficulties when operating in France. From press reports, Disney met similar culture barriers when preparing to open Euro-Disney. Japanese companies coming into the UK have in the main failed with joint UK venture organizations, but with immense care and considerable training and induction time they have managed 'shared values' with solely-owned organizations in the UK.

Harrison suggested a typology of pure cultures. Most organizations show variations of these, according to ownership, history, size, market standing and authority attributed to current senior management. He suggested four main types which he labelled power, role, task and people.[1]

POWER CULTURE
● Organizations with this type of culture tend to have been set up recently, where the originator (or the originator's family) has maintained control.
● These organizations tend to be aggressive in the market-place and can be 'hirers and firers' in relation to employees.
● If 'the boss' has charismatic power as well as ownership power, the working atmosphere can be very exciting (or threatening).
● Decision making is strictly at the top. As the organization matures, there tends to be a level of courtiers who feed 'the boss' with information he or she likes, rather than information he or she needs to know about the organization.
● The original Ford organization was a typical one with this culture.
● Organizations with this type of culture usually show considerable difficulties when the leader dies or retires.
● Succession difficulties and power culture characteristics occur in many organizations, where senior management in 'role culture' try to operate these divisions or sections as if they were the owner.

ROLE CULTURE

- Organizations with role culture tend to be large bureaucracies with several layers of management (government departments, local government, banks, multinational companies).
- Power and authority come from position in the hierarchy, not from the personal power or ownership as in the power culture.
- Positions in the hierarchy are normally achieved through specialist knowledge and experience (usually qualifications from a professional body).
- Decision making is carried out at the top of the structure. Procedural and operations manuals are normally issued (often irreverently referred to as 'the bible').
- Organizations with this type of culture are excellent for dealing with standard products or services in stable situations where decisions are made by 'rule' and not by personal whim.
- These organizations are unable to respond rapidly to changing conditions in the market-place or in society.
- All large organizations show some features of the role culture as they seek professionalism and rationality.
- These culture organizations used to supply stable career structures for their employees.

TASK CULTURE

- Organizations with a task culture approach are now becoming the norm, especially as large systems are spinning off work areas or contracting out.
- Power is based on specialist knowledge, not hierarchical position.
- Groups, mixed project groups and task forces are a feature of this culture.
- These organizations can respond very quickly to changing situations as they have very short lines of communications.
- Control from the centre is more difficult.
- People in this culture need to be able to work with other professionals and therefore need social as well as professional expertise.

PEOPLE CULTURE

- People culture organizations tend to be small and rarely survive over time.
- People come together in an organization because there are some aspects of shared values, usually where there are economies of

shared resources, or the possibilities of individual prioritized work.

● Control elements have low priority – members just want to 'do their own thing'.

● Communications are based on shared personal values.

● Small consultancies, advertising agencies, small professional groups and commune activists exhibit 'people culture' value systems.

● There are many examples of people culture in large role culture (bureaucratic) organizations, where individuals and small groups have been able to subvert resources and time to work on their private agendas rather than those of the organization.

WORKPIECE 7.3

ORGANIZATIONAL CULTURES

Consider Harrison's[1] typology of pure organizational cultures.

● From your own experience of work, social or educational organizations, try to think of examples which illustrate these types.

● If you were working in an organization, which of these cultures would you prefer?

ORGANIZATIONAL THEORIES

The study of management and organizations has developed with the emergence of the professional manager and large organization during this century. Knowledge is taken from many disciplines – economics, politics and sociology, to list a few. However, organizations as social constructs to carry out societal functions have been around for a very long time. Structures have changed as tasks and technologies have changed. As a result there are many historical commentaries and theories which have supplied leads to current practice. As it is impossible to summarize all the antecedents or even review the whole area of recent theories, it is more appropriate to look at the themes which inform current thinking.

Large organizations before the late nineteenth century tended to have a short life. Armies, for example, were created but were almost completely disbanded after the war. The military experience of organizations has contributed to modern practice – leadership best practices, line and staff, functional areas and groups, drill, training and motivation of subordinates.

The Victorian period was one of intense searching for universal principles. The arrival of more permanent large commercial and industrial organizations saw the beginning of scientific management – the search for the right structure, the right personnel with the right training to undertake the carefully measured work systems of the organizations. The search was made to find the ideal solution applicable for all organizations.

The 1914–18 war necessitated the creation of large armies and officer cadres. The new sciences of sociology and psychology were beginning to be used. However, apart from some investigations into shell-shock victims and group morale, the main inquiries were still concerned with physical measurement especially in the munitions factories – hours of work, fatigue, rest periods and the physical conditions of factory work. Some of the investigations were continued after the end of the war and at the end of the 1920s a now famous series of experiments was carried out at the Hawthorne plant of Western Electric in the USA. The results surprised the researchers. The informal organization and the behaviour of individuals as group members were rediscovered. The Human Relations movement was started in organizational studies. Studies proliferated after the second world war.

In the 1950s attempts were made to reconcile the insights of best management practice (management principles) with the insights of both scientific management and the findings of the human relations movement. The model came from biology-systems theory, a radical departure from the nineteenth-century engineering model. Organizations are seen as living structures and as such go through the same phases as individual humans.

While this summary is presented in chronological order, the ideas of the various theories are still working in our society. A systems model was used to introduce this chapter and the reader is referred to the Further Reading section for summaries of the work of the main commentators and theorists.

SUMMARY

Organizations are social units or human groupings deliberately constructed to carry out specific tasks. They can change their form, or disappear altogether, as people's wants and needs are satisfied in cheaper or better ways by alternative organizations. Small businesses are born and die according to their success or failure. Many fail to survive the death of their original founder. Some manage to become stable family-owned businesses and just a few grow into mighty companies.

Two major questions need to be asked of any organization. How effective is it? (Does it actually do what it was set up to do?) How efficient is it? (Does it make maximum use out of its resources?) Assets used by organizations have alternative uses; if they are underused there is a net loss to the community as a whole.

All organizations, no matter how large or complex, can be viewed as operating along four axes: 'task', 'people', 'organization' and 'technology'. These axes interact and a change in one necessitates changes in the other three. As an organization begins to grow, the need for specialists and the shape of the organization may begin to change. The shape of an organization and its internal structure will depend on how it has responded to the threats and opportunities in its environment. Most organizations start small with one or two people. If the organization expands, it is likely to develop supervisory levels of management. If it continues to grow, it may eventually organize itself into functional areas and specialist departments, each with its own functional manager and management hierarchy. Large organizations have in the past tended to produce tall organizational structures. Such structures can lead to communication problems, with the top management remote from what actually happens.

In the built environment many large organizations have responded by introducing an element of decentralization. Others, faced with the increasing complexity of tasks and the need to bring together specialists from several functional areas, have developed matrix forms of project organization. With the increase in information technology many organizations are being re-engineered or 'de-layered'. Head offices are disappearing into shells and employing fewer people directly. Specialists and professionals are increasingly working on short-term contracts or for fees and operating from a home base rather than from an office.

We cannot all become home-based networkers and may not all wish to be so. Taking part in the social aspects of work is often an important part of employment. Our feelings, hopes and fears, likes and dislikes are not left behind in the outside world when we work in an organization. Groupings of like-minded and like-feeling people tend to come together, with informal networks permeating the whole organization.

An organizational chart will only give the formal structure and will not explain how people behave in an organization or how they feel about working within it. Organizations develop distinctive cultures which vary with ownership, size, history, market, standing and authority accorded to senior management. Harrison[1] has suggested a typology of four pure organizational cultures: power, role, task and people.

- Draw a general model of an organization showing four interrelating axes.
- How can technology influence the ways in which goods and services are produced?
- How might the organizational structure of a small business change if it becomes successful and expands?
- Why do large organizations tend to develop 'tall structures'?
- Why might an organization decide to decentralize?
- What are the main features of the organizational cultures identified by Harrison?

REFERENCE

1.   Harrison, R. (1975) *Annual Handbook for Group Facilitators*, University Associated Inc., California.

FURTHER READING

Brunsdon, J. (1985) *The Nature of Management*, 2nd edn, Northwick Publishers.

Handy, C. (1988) *Understanding Organizations*, 3rd edn, Penguin Books.

Handy, C. (1994) *The Empty Raincoat*, Hutchinson.

Lawton, A. and Rose, A. (1991) *Organization and Management in the Public Sector*, Pitman Publishing.

Pugh, D.S. (1990) *Organization Theory: Selected Readings*, 3rd edn, Penguin Books.

Pugh, D.S., Hickson, D.J. and Hinings, C.R. (1982) *Writers on Organizations*, 3rd edn, Penguin Books.

THE ORGANIZATION OF BUSINESS IN THE BUILT ENVIRONMENT

BARRY HAMPSON

THEME

Built environment practitioners are, by definition, technicians in their own particular fields and specialities. All practitioners during the course of their professional work will encounter the need to understand the ways in which business organizes itself and operates. Each business is different, and it is essential to be able to identify well managed and financially strong businesses from their weaker counterparts. An understanding of accounts will be necessary as part of professional life since these are the principal yardstick by which the relative performance of a business is measured.

This chapter concentrates on such matters and aims to give an overview of the topics discussed.

OBJECTIVES

After reading this chapter you should be able to:

● understand different forms of business organization;

● understand the difference between fixed and working capital and between internal and external finance;

● have a knowledge of sources and methods of funding;

● define assets and liabilities with their appropriate subdivisions;

● understand the need for record keeping and budgetary control;

● understand profit and loss accounts;

● understand the main principles of marketing;

● have a knowledge of the components of the marketing mix.

Businesses in the UK are structured in a variety of ways. Particular structures are best suited to particular situations and certain options may not be available to a given situation. In addition to the options discussed in this chapter, students need to be aware that there are other structures available. For example, a local government authority is a business unit established by Act of Parliament and is also subject to the disciplines and requirements of business management.

Accurate record keeping is a prerequisite in the management of a business unit. The Inland Revenue requires accurate returns of profits to ensure that tax liabilities are correctly assessed and there are severe penalties for those who ignore this requirement. Businesses regulated under the Companies Acts are required to maintain such records so as to be able to ascertain their financial position at any time. A simple, basic record of monies received and paid is insufficient for all but the smallest business units, since larger business units need to track other aspects of their business such as unpaid accounts and need to set up appropriate financial recording systems. Socially there are increasing needs to make sure that businesses accurately account for their activities. Many larger companies now are spread over such wide areas of operation that their accounting systems have to be sophisticated so as to ensure that all transactions are captured, and so that fraud can be prevented or at least easily detected. Many larger businesses also operate profit-related pay schemes for their directors and some of their staff; the accurate quantification of profits is essential in order to enable payments under the scheme to be made.

Before discussing the forms of business it is necessary to consider the basic **double-entry bookkeeping** system which businesses use to account for their activities in financial terms and to measure their performance (Figure 8.1). The concept was developed by an Italian, Luca

Pacioli, and first published in 1494 in Venice, but the concept was not widely adopted in western Europe until the early part of the nineteenth century. The basic principles require that every accounting entry (known as debits and credits) must be matched by an equivalent entry on the opposite side. A detailed discussion of the concept of double entry bookkeeping may be found in any accounting text.

The easiest way of explaining the concept is to start from the record of a bank account. As will be seen later, a bank balance is an asset of an enterprise and the payment of wages (of, say, £100) from that bank account will cause the bank balance of the business to be depleted. To record this transaction the business will make an entry in the bank account (often referred to as a cash book) to credit, or reduce, the account by £100. The double entry will be to make a debit entry in the wages account for the same amount.

	Debits	Credits
Balance sheet:	Assets	Liabilities
Profit and loss account:	Expenses	Income

Figure 8.1 The ground rules for double-entry bookkeeping.

Businesses need to plan financial matters as much as any other decision that they make, and such plans are often prepared before the beginning of each accounting period, as a forecast of the expenditure that is likely to be incurred, as well as projecting the levels of sales required to ensure that an acceptable level of profitability is achieved. These plans are referred to as **budgets** and enable a business unit to plan and monitor progress against a benchmark, so that corrective action can be taken if necessary. The budget is set out in a similar form to the annual accounts. Regular accounts, for internal use only, are prepared at regular monthly or quarterly intervals to allow comparisons to be made. In a larger organization, the budget also allows for spending decisions to be delegated against the pre-set criteria of the budget.

As we have seen already, financial performance is separate from the flow of cash through the organization. **A cash budget** is usually prepared in addition so allowing cash resources and needs to be planned in greater detail.

Figure 8.2 outlines the principal business structures in the UK – sole traders, partnerships and limited companies.

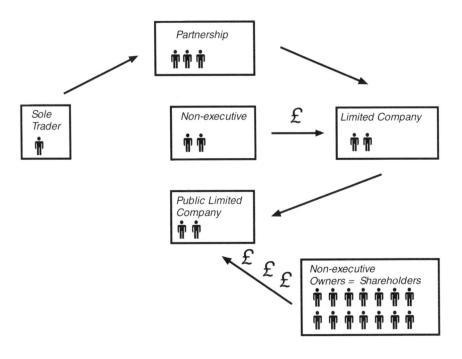

Figure 8.2 The development of business structures operating in the UK. Figures in the boxes represent owner/managers.

SOLE TRADER

This is the simplest business unit. In its base form it involves the business owner (the proprietor) simply adopting a trading name or style and offering goods or services for sale to others. The proprietor's income from the business is deemed to be the profit or loss arising in each year, and liability to third parties is generally unlimited, potentially putting at risk all assets owned by the proprietor. Many small businesses structured in this way provide services to the built environment, particularly in the construction industry.

PARTNERSHIP

This structure is a development from the sole trader position except that there are two or more 'partners' who are the proprietors of the business. It is generally advisable for the business to be governed by a partnership agreement which will cover, inter alia, matters such as sharing of profits and losses, capital contributions, winding up of the business, the records to be maintained and the duties of the partners. In the event of a dispute not covered by the agreement, or in the absence of any agreement at all, legislation known as the Partnership Act 1890 is used to settle the dispute. Many firms of quantity surveyors, architects and engineers are structured in this way.

LIMITED COMPANY

As the name implies, the liability of the **shareholders** (or members) of the company is limited to the amount invested in the company by the purchase of shares. There must be at least two shares issued and, subject to the company's constitution, there is no limit to the number of shares that can be held by any one shareholder.

When the company is formed it adopts a constitution, known as the **Memorandum and Articles of Association**, which sets down the rules by which the company is operated. In addition the company must comply with the requirements of the Companies Acts and file accounts (which may in certain circumstances be abbreviated) each year on a public register to a specified timescale.

Shareholders do not necessarily have to work in the business and this is seen as an advantage of this particular structure. Profits may be distributed to shareholders, who appoint a **Board of Directors** to manage the affairs of the company on a day-to-day basis.

A **company secretary** must also be appointed. Shareholders are able to exercise control through annual meetings which the company secretary must convene. The directors (in their capacity as directors) are treated as employees of the company and their remuneration is subject to disclosure in the annual accounts. A director may also be a shareholder.

There are two distinct forms of limited company – private and public. The difference can be detected immediately from the company name which, in the case of a **private company**, must include the word 'limited', sometimes abbreviated to 'Ltd'. **Public companies** use the abbreviation 'PLC', standing for Public Limited Company. To qualify as a PLC the company must adopt a specific form of constitution, have an issued share capital of at least £50 000 and have at least 50 members. Shares in a public limited company may be quoted and traded on the Stock Exchange, subject to the company meeting very strict Stock Exchange requirements.

Accountability to the shareholders is reinforced by law which requires the annual accounts of every company to be set out in prescribed format, to contain detailed disclosures of certain specified financial information and to be audited by an independent registered auditor. Each shareholder must be sent a copy each year. The audit requirement is relaxed for very small companies (those defined as having a turnover – or sales – of less than £350 000 per annum), provided that the shareholders agree.

In the event of a dissolution (liquidation), shareholders are entitled to share in any surplus but, provided that they have paid the nominal value of their shares, they are not liable to contribute further in the event of a deficiency. There are exceptions to this general principle in respect of director shareholders when it can be shown that the director allowed the company to continue trading when he or she knew (or ought to have known) that it was at that time insolvent (i.e. the company was unable to pay its debts as they fell due for payment) (Insolvency Act 1986).

In the built environment an additional business unit frequently found is the **housing association**. This is usually a limited liability organization registered with the Registrar of Friendly Societies; however, the shares carry no right to dividend or profit and may not be traded, and no member may hold more than one share. Requirements regarding the constitution, auditing of accounts and the conduct of the business are broadly similar to those imposed on companies.

WORKPIECE 8.1

BUSINESS STRUCTURE

A surveyor, an architect and an engineer, who are all currently employed with separate large professional practices, are considering leaving their respective firms to form a multi-disciplinary practice. What factors would they need to take into account in deciding the appropriate structure for their business?

CAPITAL AND RESERVES

FIXED WORKING CAPITAL

In order to function, a business requires **capital,** which can be provided in a number of ways. In consideration of its structure and operation, a business must be viewed separately and distinctly from the owners and managers themselves. This is sometimes referred to as the **entity concept.** The fixed capital is normally provided by way of shares in limited companies, and by cash or other assets for sole traders and partnerships.

Capital can be computed as being the excess of the assets over the liabilities of the business, and will include accumulated but undistributed profits. The principle of double-entry bookkeeping means that the liabilities added to the capital will equate with the assets of the enterprise. The description of capital will vary according to each entity. A limited company's capital will appear as **share capital**; sole traders and partnerships will simply describe it as **capital accounts**.

As a broad definition the capital may be described as the initial sum invested in the enterprise to provide the means by which it can begin to trade and operate. As each accounting period elapses the business will generate a profit or a loss. Accumulated profits are called **reserves,** and in accounting periods where losses are incurred those losses will be deducted from the accumulated reserves. During the life of a business there will often be times when the capital needs to be increased, perhaps to help finance expansion. Capital is, therefore, seldom a static part of any business.

Working capital describes the capital that the business needs to maintain in liquid or near-liquid form to enable it to meet day-to-day requirements, to allow it to continue to operate by paying suppliers and other creditors whilst waiting for debts to be collected, and for stocks to be liquidated. The working capital of the business increases in line with the base of its activity and is calculated from the balance sheet by deducting current liabilities from current assets. Financial analysts look for a ratio of current assets to current liabilities of at least 1:1. The higher the ratio, the better placed the entity is to withstand sudden and unexpected demands on its resources.

SOURCES OF FINANCE AND METHODS OF FUNDING

Finance is available from many sources and may be raised in many forms. Raising finance is very much driven by the purpose for which that finance will be required, and the life expectancy of the project. For example, a housing association will not raise overdraft finance for the very long-term funding of the development of a new estate which will provide homes for rent for the next 30 years. Conversely, an architect's practice will not take out a 25-year loan to finance the acquisition of a computer-aided design system, which can have an economic life of as little as 3 years. Small business and professional practices are often heavily dependent upon overdrafts from the major clearing banks, simply because they are unable to raise finance competitively elsewhere.

In addition to the traditional forms of finance, the 1980s saw the emergence of the **leasing** industry, as a way of funding capital purchases of equipment. This form of funding can be either an 'operating' or a 'finance' lease. Under an **operating lease,** a rental is paid for as long as the capital item is in use, whereas a **finance lease** normally provides for a fixed rental to be paid for a specific period, with a lower (or secondary) rental, usually of a fairly nominal amount, to allow the business to continue to use the asset. Taxation legislation prohibits the sale of a leased asset directly to the lessee at the end of the term, but it can be sold to an unconnected third party, who can immediately sell it on to the original lessee. You will often see operating leases referred to as '**off balance sheet finance**', since the assets and the corresponding liabilities are not shown in the books of the business, as the assets are not (and never can be) the legal property of the lessee, unless a further transaction involving an unconnected party intervenes.

Hire purchase, which became relatively unpopular during the growth in leasing, is now finding favour again. A hire purchase agreement, as its name implies, provides for a business to acquire ownership of an asset after a period of hire. The contract is written so that legal ownership passes with the payment of the final instalment due under the contract. The legal owner is entitled to seize or repossess the goods if payments are in default.

Figure 8.3 illustrates some of the appropriate sources of funding for an enterprise, and some of the advantages and disadvantages involved.

Financial accounting based on the double-entry theory is founded upon 10 fundamental concepts:

**ASSETS AND
LIABILITIES**

1. Entity – to distinguish and segregate the business or entity from its owners.
2. Money measurement – the accounting tradition of only including items which can be expressed in monetary terms.
3. Going concern – the presumption that the entity is ongoing and not on the verge of cessation.
4. Cost – the practice of including items in accounts by reference to their cost as distinct from their value.
5. Realization – profits are recognized only when assets of the business are sold.
6. Accruals – distinguishing the right to convert an asset or liability into cash, from the receipt or payment of the cash itself.
7. Matching – ensuring that income is linked (matched) with the associated expenses of earning that income.

(a)

Type of finance	Source of finance				
	Pension funds	Insurance companies	Building societies	Merchant banks	Clearing banks
Overdraft	No	No	No	Yes	Yes
Development loan	No	No	Yes	Yes	Yes
Deferred interest loan	No	Some	Yes	Some	Some
Index-linked loan	Yes	Yes	Some	No	No
Fixed rate loans	Some	Yes	Some	Yes	Yes
Stepped interest fixed rate	Yes	Yes	No	No	No
Loan stock	Yes	Yes	No	No	No
Structured bank loan	No	No	No	Yes	Some

Please note that this table suggests *likely* sources of finance of the various types. Some products are only available in limited quantities and not all are available all the time (for example, index-linked loans have been virtually unheard of recently as a result of falling inflation expectations)

Key:
Yes = Normally readily available when product is available
No = Rarely available, if at all
Some = Limited availability when product is available.

(b)

	Advantages	Disadvantages
Variable rate borrowing		
Building societies	Longer loan periods Some control of interest rates Some flexibility Relatively low initial fees Early redemption possible without high penalty Will deal direct with Borrower	Limited funds availability Higher base rate Margin over Building Society or LIBOR base Advances only available against valuation Must be a first fixed charge
Banks	Wide availability Wide choice and flexibility of structure Lower pricing and initial costs Flexibility on security Early redemption penalties rare Further advances available	Shorter initial loan periods More volatile interest rates
Fixed rate borrowing	Known costs Recommended for use when interest rates are low	Available more scarcely when interest rates are low Cost for early redemption Normally only available against first fixed charges
Stock/bond issues	Fixed interest rates Long loan period Marketability Some flexibility of structure (e.g. issue at a discount) Possible tax benefits to lender	High initial price because of limited marketability and complex structure Borrower must be substantial Possible timing difficulties Higher level of security May require investment return on sinking fund with inherent associated risks Rigid long-term structure
Index linked	Low start repayments Long period availability Ideal in low inflation periods	Limited availability Heavy early redemption penalties Potentially inflexible Potentially disastrous results if inflation is high in early years

Figure 8.3 Funding: (a) likely sources of funds; (b) advantages and disadvantages of types of funding for long-term projects.

FUNDING

A housing association is looking to raise finance to meet the long-term funding requirements of its development programme. These are estimated to be £10 million over the next three years. Consider the risk factors involved and recommend the types of funding that the organization should consider, and which organizations should be approached for funding.

8. Periodicity – making periodic reports to the owners of the business, normally annually.

9. Consistency – ensuring that accounting principles are applied evenly so that meaningful comparisons can be drawn between periods.

10. Prudence – accounting generally assumes profits to be deferred until earned, but expenses or losses to be recognized as soon as they are anticipated.

These concepts cannot be considered in detail here and students are referred to Glautier and Underdown.[1]

In considering assets and liabilities, the concepts of cost and realization require further clarification. Accountants use monetary values to express financial transactions, and it is the original **cost** of an item which determines its expression in accounts (often referred to as **'financial statements'** because of the greater detail now being reported). Before considering this concept further it is necessary to consider how we define assets and liabilities (Figure 8.4)

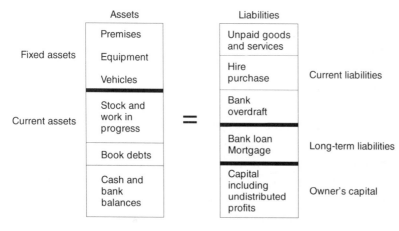

Figure 8.4 Assets and liabilities.

In our own lives we regard anything that we own as an asset – a car, a house, cash, bank deposits, books, hi-fi equipment etc. In business accounting terms **assets** may be defined as items, capable of being expressed in monetary terms, which have a value to the business entity. At the lowest level a subcontractor's wheelbarrow is an asset of his trade, in the same way (at the opposite end of the spectrum) as the vast cash and bank deposits amassed by GEC. In financial reporting terms those assets are then classified into two main categories: fixed and current.

Current assets are those which are held in cash or near-cash (sometimes referred to as '**liquid**') form. For example, a bank balance is a current asset, as is an unpaid sales invoice, since there is a presumption that the invoice will be paid (or converted into cash). Convention dictates that an asset which cannot be readily converted into cash (liquidated) within one year is not a current asset.

Fixed assets are those assets which are acquired with a view to producing returns to the entity for a time which exceeds one reporting period. For example, a builders' merchant will purchase a lorry to enable the delivery of materials to customers' sites. The expectation is that this asset will have a life of several years, although it is recognized that the life of the vehicle is finite. If the lorry is paid for using cash (say, £20 000) in the entity's bank account, the current asset (cash) is converted into a fixed asset (the lorry) and will be shown in the books of the business at a value of £20 000. It is accepted, however, that two things immediately occur as the builders' merchant takes delivery of the lorry and begins to use it to make deliveries. Firstly the vehicle begins to wear out, and it acquires a second-hand or **realizable value** significantly lower than its original cost price, and secondly it begins to incur cost in use (**running costs**) which are necessary for the asset to deliver ongoing use to the business. These running expenses do not add to the value of the asset, and are charged to the profit and loss account (see next section).

Accountants have devised a method of dealing with the reduction in value of the life of the asset which is known as **depreciation.** This charges the gradual decline in value of the asset as an expense to the profit and loss account over its expected economic life, but the technique involves a degree of estimation and forecasting. Returning to our example of the builders' merchant and the lorry, let us assume that the merchant expects a 7-year life from this investment, and projects a second-hand value at the end of the 7th year of £2500. The technique of depreciation will charge £2500 of the cost of the asset (i.e. the cost will be reduced by £2500 each year) against the profits of the business (Figure 8.5).

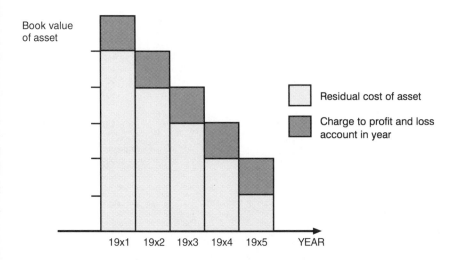

Figure 8.5   Assets and residual costs.

Depreciation does not attempt to portray the asset each year at its market or second-hand value, since the concept of 'going concern' presumes that the business will continue for the projected 7-year life of the asset, and the matching concept justifies the spreading of the reduction in value of the asset over the period that it is at work in the business.

The opposite of assets is **liabilities,** which are those items that require the entity to make a payment of cash at some point in the future. A bank overdraft is a liability, since the bank will require the payment of money into the overdrawn account at some point. An unpaid bill for goods or services is also a liability. Like assets, liabilities are classified in the reporting entity's financial statements, distinguishing between current (those requiring payment within one year) and long-term liabilities. **Current liabilities** are those payable within one year from the reporting date, such as taxes, trade creditors and bank overdrafts, whilst **long-term liabilities** are those such as bank loans payable at a predetermined point in the future. The prudence concept requires entities to acknowledge liabilities as soon as they are thought to exist and this can present major problems for some entities operating within the built environment such as large-scale contractors. For example, the claims for expenses and delay by the various Channel Tunnel contractors will take many years to resolve, and attributing a monetary value to them for inclusion in financial statements in the meantime will be a near impossible task (Figure 8.6).

	Balance sheets			
	Company One		Company Two	
	31:21:×1	31:12:×2	31:3:×2	31:3:×3
Fixed assets	11, 650,000	23,800,000	14,650,000	15,100,000
Current assets				
Stock	2,500,000	200,000	2,000,000	3,000,000
Debtors	2,750,000	2,500,000	2,500,000	3,000,000
Cash	4,400,000	—	300,000	500,000
	9,650,000	2,700,000	4,800,000	6,500,000
Current liabilities				
Creditors	4,800,000	5,800,000	2,750,000	3,300,000
Bank overdraft	—	2,200,000	—	—
Taxation	1,250,000	750,000	800,000	350,000
Proposed dividend	250,000	450,000	450,000	550,000
	6,300,000	9,200,000	4,000,000	4,200,000
Net current assets				
	3,350,000	(6,500,000)	800,000	2,300,000
Long-term loans				
	(1,000,000)	(3,000,000)	(7,000,000)	(8,000,000)
Net assets				
	14,000,000	14,300,000	8,450,000	9,400,000
Financed by				
Share capital	10,000,000	10,000,000	5,500,000	6,500,000
Reserves	4,000,000	4,300,000	2,950,000	2,900,000
	14,000,000	14,300,000	8,450,000	9,400,000

Figure 8.6   Balance sheets.

THE PROFIT AND LOSS ACCOUNT

The profit and loss account is the second of the two primary statements in financial reporting, and is used to show the performance of the business over a particular period, usually one year. Figure 8.7 depicts a simple example.

Of the concepts referred to earlier in this chapter, the accruals concept is particularly relevant in computing the profit and loss account, since expenses include those incurred but unpaid, and revenues include those earned but not yet received.

Wendover Building
Profit and loss account year ended 31 December 19x1

Sales = Work done			30,000
Expenses –	Materials	7,500	
	Wages	12,500	
	Less: closing stock	1,500	
	Cost of sales	18,500	
	Indirect costs:		
	Rent of yard	1,500	
	Office salaries	2,000	
	Depreciation of lorry	3,500	25,500
	Net profit		4,500

Figure 8.7 Profit and loss account for Wendover Building.

The profit and loss account interacts with the balance sheet and this can be illustrated in the example in Figure 8.8 with balance sheets at the start and end of the financial period. (We have assumed that current assets and liabilities remain unchanged.)

Wendover Building
Balance sheet

	At 1 January 19x1		At 31 December 19x1	
Fixed assets – lorry at cost		14,000		10,500
Current assets				
Stocks	–		1,500	
Debtors	6,100		4,600	
Cash and bank balances	1,400		1,400	
	7,500		**7,500**	
Current liabilities				
Creditors	2,600		2,600	
Bank loan	4,600		4,600	
	7,200		**7,200**	
Net current assets		300		300
Net assets		**14,300**		**10,800**
Capital account				
Balance brought forward		**14,300**		14,300
Profit for year				5,000
				19,300
Less drawings				8,500
				10,800

Figure 8.8 Balance sheet for Wendover Building.

151

Like the balance sheet, the profit and loss account is divided into subclassifications. **Income** is normally shown at the head, with income from the main business activity achieving prominence. Income from the business's mainstream activity is normally known as **turnover.** Ancillary business income, such as interest accruing from the temporary investment of funds, is usually given a lower priority.

WORKPIECE 8.3

BALANCE SHEET

The Designitwell Architectural Practice has the following balances in its books at the end of December. Update the balances from the information shown in the notes, and draft into an appropriate profit and loss balance sheet format.

	£	£
Debtors and Creditors	7,400	12,200
Office Premises	35,000	
Office Equipment	15,000	
Sales		80,000
Opening work in progress	2,600	
Staff Salaries	32,000	
Electricity and gas	2,300	
Telephone	3,600	
Business Rates	5,100	
Drawings	35,000	
Bank Balance	17,000	
Bank Loan		34,000
Capital Account		18,800
TOTAL	145,000	145,000

Notes:

1. Depreciation is to be calculated at 20% on the office equipment.

2. Closing work in progress is valued at £4,300.

The second classification involves costs which vary directly in proportion to volumes of sales. These costs are often described as **direct costs** or **cost of sales.** Typically they will be materials and the production cost of labour. In a manufacturing or construction environment such costs will vary in proportion to turnover or sales. For example, the business will only incur costs of materials when it has actually won contracts to carry out work, and will only engage bricklayers or similar tradesmen when there is work for them to do.

The valuation of stock and work in progress will feature in the cost-of-sales part of the profit and loss account. There are a number of ways of valuing stocks and work in progress, and accountants have always argued amongst themselves over this particular issue. Accounting standards have somewhat reduced the scope for debate, and the stocks and work in progress of a business are valued at the lower of their cost, or their **net realizable value.**

The annual **stock-take** or count generates the raw data from which the valuation is compiled. At the end of each accounting period the stock valuation forms one of the assets of the enterprise and becomes a cost charged into the profit and loss account of the ensuing period. The valuation at the close of the period becomes a deduction from the costs incurred during the period. The Wendover Building example given above illustrates the principles and the presentation typically followed.

The turnover, less the cost of sales, is known as **gross profit** and is referred to by readers of accounts wishing to make comparisons between business entities. The gross profit (or **gross margin**) percentage is expressed as the gross profit earned divided by the turnover.

The third classification normally followed is that of **indirect costs**, sometimes referred to as **overheads.** These will include costs associated with the business which are relatively inflexible and tend not to vary significantly with changes in the level of activity of the business or enterprise. An example often quoted is that of office accommodation costs. An architect's practice will occupy offices, often rented, on a long-term basis at a fixed annual rental. Whether the fees earned by the practice are £25 or £25 000 in the year the rent will not vary.

Further classifications are often included for other types of income and expenditure, such as interest income, and dividends paid to shareholders.

Various other ratios and indicators are often computed from the profit and loss account by readers and users of the accounts. This is made easier by entities reporting on a public basis such as limited companies and Friendly Societies where accounts are generally available, but is more difficult with partnerships and sole traders who do not have to file accounts publicly. Those organizations regulated by statute also generally have to comply with standardized accounting and reporting formats, which means that the information they have to disclose is set out in a standardized format, facilitating easier comparison between business entities.

WORKPIECE 8.4

UNDERSTANDING PROFIT AND LOSS ACCOUNTS

You have before you the last 2 years' profit and loss accounts of two companies which are being considered for a £3 million contract (to run over 10 months) to build a new housing scheme for a local housing association. Summarize the financial strengths and weaknesses of each candidate.

| | Profit and Loss Account | | | |
| | Company A | | Company B | |
	Year 1	Year 2	Year 1	Year 2
Turnover	16,000,000	13,000,000	14,000,000	20,000,000
Cost of sales	**8,500,000**	**6,500,000**	**7,000,000**	**12,000,000**
Gross profit	7,500,000	6,500,000	7,000,000	6,000,000
Distribution costs	800,000	700,000	1,200,000	900,000
Admin. costs	**3,200,000**	**3,300,000**	**3,000,000**	**3,300,000**
Operating profit	3,500,000	2,500,000	2,800,000	1,800,000
Interest income	250,000	100,000	100,000	50,000
Interest expense	**750,000**	**800,000**	**800,000**	**1,000,000**
Profit before tax	3,000,000	1,800,000	2,100,000	850,000
Taxation	**1,250,000**	**750,000**	**800,000**	**350,000**
Profit after tax	1,750,000	1,050,000	1,300,000	500,000
Dividends	750,000	750,000	450,000	550,000
Accum. profits b/fwd	**3,000,000**	**4,000,000**	**2,000,000**	**2,950,000**
Accum. profits c/fwd	**4,000,000**	**4,300,000**	**2,950,000**	**2,900,000**

MARKETING

Businesses promote themselves through marketing. Marketing is distinguished from selling as it concentrates on development of the market for the company's products as a whole, whilst sales concentrates on targeting a particular product from a range offered by a business to meet a particular need of a client or customer. For example, a brick manufacturer markets its products by increasing awareness of the range of facings and strengths available to a whole range of outlets. This will include advertising, research of competitors' products and after-sales service. On the other hand, sales involve the act of identifying a particular product from the company's range to meet a given situation and the act of negotiating a particular sale. Some companies employ marketing strategies that are so effective that the products sell themselves; often-quoted examples include Coca Cola and McDonalds.

As mentioned earlier, the business entity, in its budget setting, has a required level of sales activity for its output, but demand from customers may vary through a number of phases from non-existent through irregular to full, or even excess levels. Marketing theory allows the management of business entities to take steps to react to these constantly changing conditions. Marketing strategies allow businesses to plan their strategies and to maximize consumption, consumer satisfaction, choice and quality of life. The maintenance of these elements in a balanced state is what the marketeer strives to achieve, and is now widely practised throughout the commercial sector in both the business and non-profit divisions.

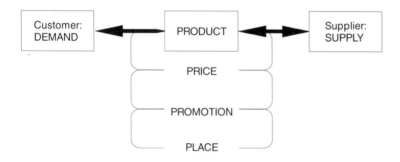

Figure 8.9 Influencing factors.

The core concepts of marketing are needs, wants, demands, products exchange transactions and markets, and they are guided by five philosophies (Figure 8.9):

● The product cost concept theorizes that consumers favour products available at a low cost and that the responsibility of management is to minimize prices by maximizing production efficiency.
● The product quality theory indicates that consumers prefer quality products and that the quality of the product is sufficient.
● The selling concept suggests that consumer behaviour is driven by large-scale sales and promotion activity.
● The marketing concept suggests that organizations should research their own defined markets and supply specified solutions.
● The societal marketing concept requires companies or organizations to generate customer satisfaction.

Business entities develop overall marketing strategues by developing positioning strategies, by deciding which markets they wish to enter and targeting segments within those markets. (A **market segment** is defined as a group of consumers who respond similarly to a given set of stimuli). The **marketing mix** (Figure 8.10) is the technique used to identify the variables to produce the required response in the target markets. These variables are often referred to as the 'four Ps' – product, price, place and promotion.

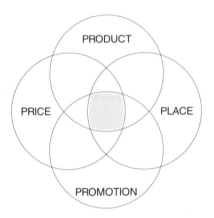

Figure 8.10 The marketing mix. The shaded area represents the optimum market.

Product refers to the item or items being marketed – for each building site a developer will decide whether to offer 5-bedroom executive homes, or single-bedroom starter homes. The product includes all ancillary elements of the package on offer, including after-sales service and warranties.

Price is the amount to be paid for the product, and may often be flexible to attract prospective purchasers – our developer may offer subsidized mortgages for a period, or 'free' legal fees or a range of kitchen appliances, to make his product apparently more attractive than that of any competitors.

Place refers to activities of the business unit to make the products available. The developer may well operate on a national scale and be able to offer part-exchange schemes.

Promotion represents activities by the market maker that extol the virtues of the product involved and persuade prospective purchasers to buy or consume. This will include corporate brochures, advertising and special promotional activities as incentives to stimulate consumer activity.

The marketing programme will blend these elements to help the entity achieve its stated marketing goals.

MARKETING STRATEGY

You are the marketing manager for a developer who has acquired a site on the edge of a major industrial town in the north-east of England.

The developer has the ability to develop three possible styles of home:

● warden-controlled sheltered accommodation for the elderly to rent;
● starter homes to be sold on shared ownership terms in partnership with a local housing association;
● large executive family homes for outright sale.

Identify the additional information that you would take into account in formulating a recommendation to the directors as to the type of housing to be developed and what strategies you would adopt in formulating a marketing strategy for the chosen housing type. Try to identify potential sources of the information you require.

Don't read any further until you have completed this.

SUGGESTED SOLUTION

Additional information required would include:

Information	Source
● Analysis of local employment	Local council
● Age profile of local population	Previous census
● Local pay information	Local council/census
● Location of site in relation to amenities, e.g. schools, shops, bus and rail services, churches	Map
● Prospects for growth	
● Relative profitability of each housing type	Your employer
● Demand for housing	Local council
● Availability of potential experienced housing association partner	Local council
● Location of site in relation to local topography	Map

In this chapter we have discussed how business entities within the built environment are organized, and how they are required to account for their activities. In this regard we have examined the principles of accounting, and considered the difference in that regard between capital and revenue expenditure and income.

Students will have considered, and should be able to interpret, the profit and loss account and balance sheet of an enterprise, although it is emphasized that the examples cited are relatively simplistic. Further study will be required if students wish to acquire a greater depth of skills.

The expenditure base of an organization, and its need to generate income to achieve a projected or budget position, led us to question how the organization seeks to produce that sales income and to examine the basic principles of marketing and the components of the marketing mix.

CHECKLIST OF POINTS

- Why do business units need to keep accounts?
- What factors need to be considered in deciding upon an appropriate structure for a business?
- What is the difference between 'fixed capital' and 'working capital'?
- What factors might need to be considered in choosing a method of funding?
- What are the 10 'fundamental concepts' which underpin the double-entry method of financial accounting?
- What is meant by the terms 'cost', 'fixed assets', 'current assets', 'depreciation' and 'current liabilities'?
- How does a profit and loss account interact with a balance sheet?
- What elements might a 'marketeer' wish to keep in a balance sheet?
- What are the four elements of the marketing mix?

REFERENCE

1. Glautier, M.W.E. and Underdown, B. (1984) *Accounting Theory and Practice*, 5th edn, Pitman, London.

FURTHER READING

Coombs, H.M. and Jenkins, D.E. (1991) *Public Sector Financial Management*, Chapman & Hall.
Lee, G.A. (1990) *Modern Financial Accounting*, Chapman & Hall.

MANAGING PEOPLE IN BUILT ENVIRONMENT ORGANIZATIONS

CHAPTER NINE

TASH KHAN

This chapter is concerned with exploring the operation and requirements of the personnel function found in major built environment organizations. The approach will be to examine the development of personnel management and then look closely at the operation of the personnel function in two principal areas: employee resourcing and employee development.

THEME

After reading this chapter you should be able to:

OBJECTIVES

● describe the main stages in the historical development of the personnel function;

● discuss the meaning of the terms personnel management and human resource management;

● describe the process of recruitment, selection, induction, training and appraisal.

It is worthwhile beginning by looking at the historical development of personnel management, as it helps to identify some of the enduring concerns and provides a starting point to understanding the various functions of personnel. Torrington[1] describes the following stages in the development of personnel from the nineteenth century to the present.

INTRODUCTION

DEVELOPMENT OF PERSONNEL MANAGEMENT

THE SOCIAL REFORMER At the beginning of the nineteenth century, there were those who intervened in industrial affairs to support severely underprivileged factory workers. Reformers like Lord Shaftesbury and Robert Owen criticized employer behaviour and influenced the appointment, for the first time, of individuals in the workplace who were responsible for personnel.

THE ACOLYTE OF BENEVOLENCE Motivated by the Christian charity of paternalist employers like the Quaker families of Cadbury, Rowntree and the Lever Brothers, welfare officers were appointed with specific responsibility for improving the lot of the employees. This included setting up schemes of unemployment benefit, sick pay and subsidized housing for their employees. The Institute of Welfare Officers (now the Institute of Personnel Management) was established in 1913. This concern for welfare is still a persistent theme in personnel today.

THE HUMANE BUREAUCRAT The increase in the size of organizations in the 1920s and 1930s was accompanied by specialization in management and the shop floor. The personnel manager became increasingly concerned with role specification, selection, training and placement. Within the construction industry, not only specialization but also a greater variety of ways of organizing the process of construction put greater emphasis on these activities. Thus the personnel manager served organizational rather than paternalist employer objectives. Most of the activities of personnel management that developed during this time remain central to personnel today.

THE CONSENSUS NEGOTIATOR As a result of full employment and steady growth after the second world war, trade union assertiveness brought a shift towards bargaining by the employer. This led to a 'substantial increase in general in the degree of specialization of industrial relations in the workplace'[2], which added a further dimension to the skills of personnel managers.

Since that time bargaining by management in the construction industry with trade unions has been conducted through the Building Employers Confederation which represents the interests of a number of affiliated contractors. The Confederation negotiates on wage rates and conditions of employment with the unions. 'The main advantage of these arrangements for management was that they more or less excluded trade union officials from the workplace . . .'[2]. This led Fryer[3] to write: '. . . labour relations have been comparatively good in building, so most firms have not felt the need to employ industrial relations specialists. They have been slow to formulate written local policies and procedures for consulting with workers and unions.' It is also worth noting that the trade unions like the Union of Construction, Allied Trades and Technicians (UCATT) and the Transport and General Workers' Union (TGWU) represent mainly craftsmen and labourers. Negotiations on pay and conditions do not exist on a collective basis between management and 'professionals' like civil engineers, structural engineers and quantity surveyors.

ORGANIZATION MAN From the 1960s interest has focused increasingly on the effectiveness of the organization as a whole. For the personnel specialist this meant a move away from dealing with individual employees on behalf of the management, towards dealing with the programmes of organizational and management development (Chapter 10).

CURRENT DEVELOPMENTS

Increased competition and rapid changes in the market-place have led to the introduction of a number of initiatives like flexible working practices, total quality management and the division of organizations into strategic business units. Accompanying this there has been a change in the vocabulary used to describe the management of the workforce. 'Personnel management' is giving way to 'human resource management' (HRM). The debate about whether there is a substantive difference between HRM and personnel management brings into critical focus the present function of personnel management and how it contributes to an organization's goals. Let us look first at some definitions:

> Personnel management is a series of activities which first enable working people and their employing organizations to agree about the objectives and nature of their working relationships and secondly ensures that agreement is fulfilled.[4]

This definition assumes a pluralist approach to personnel management, where employees or employee representatives can in some way enter into discussion with management on issues concerned with the working relationship. Furthermore, this definition associates personnel management with activities such as selecting, developing and rewarding employees in order that the aims and objectives of the organization are achieved. Not surprisingly this view is very close to Torrington's description of the personnel managers role as a 'human bureaucrat' and 'consensus negotiator'.

On the other hand the main dimensions of HRM involve 'the goal of integration . . . the goal of employee commitment, the goal of flexibility/adaptability (i.e. organic structures, functional flexibility), the goal of quality (i.e. quality of staff, performance, standards or public image)'.[5]

This definition places human resource management at the heart of business planning. Utilizing human resources is a matter of determining and implementing 'mutually consistent policies that promote commitment and which, as a consequence, foster a willingness in employees to act flexibly.'[6] This view is essentially a unitarist one, requiring each employee to identify with the organization and its aims. HRM activities, however, still rely on a number of systems in and around the conventional theory of personnel management.[7]

There are certain similarities between these two definitions:

- Both definitions emphasize the importance of integrating personnel/HRM practices with organizational goals.
- Both definitions emphasize the importance of individuals fully developing their abilities for their personal satisfaction and to make their best contribution to the organization's success.
- Both definitions identify placing the right people into the right jobs.

The major differences are that, in personnel management, specialist personnel work has to be 'layered' on to line management's responsibilities (extrinsic influence) whereas HRM is vested in line management (intrinsic influence). In fact it is often said about HRM that it is far too important to be left to personnel specialists! Furthermore personnel management appears to be something practised on subordinates rather than experienced by management. HRM, on the other hand, with its focus on employee development, includes the development of the management team. A third difference is that most HRM models emphasize the management of the organization's culture as the central activity for senior management. In traditional personnel management 'organizational development' has proclaimed a similar aim, but it has not been considered a mainstream activity.

The client has been identified as a driving force for improvement in the construction process.[6] A good example of this is the adoption by many built environment organizations of BS 5750/ISO 9000, which is the quality assurance standard.

This, together with the greater variety and complexity of work undertaken by the construction and development teams, has resulted in a set of relationships that are much more mutually dependent than in the past, with responsibility for quality and communication being pushed further down into the workplace. Thus it becomes increasingly important for staff to be more aware of the organization's aims and objectives and typically this has resulted in management implementing quality circles, team briefs and appraisal schemes.

The language of HRM provides an interpretation of personnel management which the non-specialist can use, and helps to describe the kind of change built environment organizations are experiencing in the management of their people. More importantly, HRM puts responsibility for the delivery of personnel practices firmly in the hands of line management, which is after all where it must be practised if it is to serve any useful purpose as a management discipline.

No matter which view is taken, two main personnel functions remain clear – employee resourcing (recruitment and selection) and employee development (training, development and appraisal).

Before someone is employed, it is worthwhile establishing if there are any alternatives to recruitment, including: reorganizing the work; using overtime; using IT to mechanize the work; staggering the hours; making the job part-time; subcontracting the work or using agency staff.

If the decision is that recruitment is necessary, then there are four questions which need to be addressed:[8]

- What does the job consist of?
- In what way is it, or should it be, different from the job done by the present incumbent?
- What are the aspects of the job that specify the type of candidate?
- What are the aspects of the job that the ideal candidate wants to know before deciding to apply?

WHAT DOES THE JOB CONSIST OF, AND IN WHAT WAY IS IT DIFFERENT FROM THE JOB DONE BY THE PRESENT INCUMBENT? This is an ideal opportunity to reassess the

HOW IS THIS DEBATE REFLECTED IN THE CONTEXT OF BUILT ENVIRONMENT ORGANIZATIONS?

EMPLOYEE RESOURCING RECRUITMENT STRATEGY

DETERMINING A VACANCY

nature of the job and modify the tasks and responsibilities in order to maximize the contribution of the role. Conventionally this involves some sort of job analysis, which is a systematic process of collecting and analysing information about tasks, responsibilities and the context of the job. Sources of information include:

- The present job incumbent. Information will be biased and requires the cooperation of the individual.
- The immediate manager/supervisor. The supervisor may not have a detailed enough knowledge of the job but is in the best position to determine team/group/departmental objectives.
- Other staff. Colleagues or associates may provide job-related information from a different perspective.

The more sources of information and methods of collecting the information that are used, the more reliable will be the job analysis.

The end product of job analysis is a job description. These may vary considerably but will typically contain:

- job title, and other identifying data;
- reporting relationships;
- the purpose, aims and objectives of the job;
- the key tasks;
- the main contacts inside and outside the organization.

It is important to remember that job analysis is not a one-off exercise. Traditional features like tasks and duties, position in the hierarchy, controls and reporting relationships may need to be reviewed in order to respond to changes like de-layering of organizations, increasing recognition of project and team work and job flexibility.

WHAT ASPECTS OF THE JOB SPECIFY THE TYPE OF CANDIDATE? Answering this question will help to reduce the effects of bias and prejudice during the selection phase. A widely used aid here is Rodger's seven-point plan[4], which is a series of questions gathered under seven headings:

- physical make-up (health, physique, appearance, bearing, speech);

- attainments (education, training, experience, degree of success in each);
- general intelligence;
- special aptitudes (mechanical, numerical, verbal, drawing, music, manual dexterity);
- interests (intellectual, practical, social, artistic, physical activities);
- disposition (acceptability, influence, dependability, self-reliance);
- circumstances (domestic, family, special).

The questions are formulated to relate to people but have to be interpreted in relation to the demands of a job or occupation. The questions serve to link the form in which the job demands are specified to the way that the candidate will be assessed.

WORKPIECE 9.1

CRITERIA FOR PERSONNEL SELECTION

Use the seven-point plan to draw up a person specification for the following:

- A lecturer in construction (in either higher or further education).
- A receptionist in a hotel.

- A sales representative for building products.

Note any difficulties you experienced carrying out the exercise and discuss these with your colleagues. Analyse the similarities and differences.

WHAT ASPECTS OF THE JOB DOES THE IDEAL CANDIDATE WANT TO KNOW BEFORE APPLYING? This information will form the basis of advertising the vacancy and crucially attracting the right candidate.

SELECTION METHODS

In reality selection is a two-way process: it is as much to do with the interviewer selecting someone suitable for the job to be done, as it is to do with the prospective employee selecting the work which is being offered. Throughout the selection process the applicants choose between organizations by evaluating things like correspondence from the employer, the selection methods used and the information they gain at the interview.

APPLICATION FORMS These forms are probably the most common method of taking initial employment decisions. Recently the application form has been extended to play a more significant part in the employment process. However, it must be remembered that there are not many posts for which lengthy forms are appropriate.

Biodata or the 'personal history inventory', another form of extended application form, seeks information on the kind of experiences a person has had and involves the candidate answering a range of questions concerning personal life history and background. This is then used to build up a profile of the candidate to be measured against 'suitable' profiles of successful incumbents.

TESTING   Tests can bring more objectivity to selection decisions if they are chosen on the basis that the test scores correlate with subsequent job performance, so that a high test score would predict high job performance and a low test score would predict low job performance.

Critical features of any test used in selection are predictive validity, which is the extent to which the test can predict subsequent job behaviour, and reliability, which is the degree to which the test measures consistently whatever it does measure. Biodata, for instance, has approximately a 40% level of predictability.[9]

Torrington and Hall[4] remark that on the whole tests are not 'outstanding predictors of future performance'.

INTERVIEWING

> Employment interviewing is like sex and driving: most people rate themselves highly, the consequences of mistakes can be serious, when something goes wrong there is a tendency to blame the other party, and nonetheless most of us continue to do it. [10]

The British Psychological Society quotes predictive validity coefficients of 0.25 for structured interviews and zero for unplanned interviews. Fowler[11], identifies the main elements of a structured interview:

- Preparation – this stage involves looking for a reasonable match between the application form and the person specification and noting those features of the application which seem weakest against the specification, so that these can be probed more deeply.
- Sequence and timing of the interview – there is no best sequence but the key is to decide in advance what sequence to follow and which elements of the sequence are most important.

- Question technique – the most common advice on questioning technique is to use open questions (questions which cannot be answered by a 'yes' or 'no)'.

Other types of questions include:

- Probing questions – to provide a clearer focus to answers that are too short or too generalized.
- Closed questions – to clarify a point of fact (usually a question with a yes/no response).
- Play-back questions – testing the interviewer's understanding of what has been said (the interviewer would usually summarize what has been said in order to solicit confirmation from the interviewee).
- Hypothetical questions – putting a situation to the candidate and asking how they would respond.

WORKPIECE 9.2

SELECTION INTERVIEW

Design a series of questions to ask at a selection interview for the posts identified in Workpiece 9.1.

WORKPIECE 9.3

YOUR NEXT JOB

Imagine you are preparing for your next job interview. Using the seven-point plan, identify the criteria you think an employer would be using for a post for someone with your abilities, skills and experience.

ANALYSING THE RESULT This last stage establishes how well the information obtained matches the specification. Any judgements should be rational, explicable and uninfluenced by irrelevancies or prejudice. This is particularly important since legislation, dealing with sex and race discrimination, requires organizations to develop procedures which are defensible against the charge that applicants have been unfairly treated.

EMPLOYEE DEVELOPMENT

TRAINING AND DEVELOPMENT

From an employer's perspective 'training is associated with the process of ensuring that employees acquire the requisite knowledge and skills to perform present and future jobs in the organization'.[10] Training is also concerned with motivation, in that it involves changing employees' attitudes or approaches to tasks that they are required to perform.

There are two distinct frameworks for training in the construction industry. The first (craft/vocational training) is a national scheme administered by the Construction Industry Training Board. The second (management, supervisory and technician training) is in the main a concern for individual built environment organizations.

Because of differences in the context and scope of how they are managed, craft/vocational training and management training are examined separately.

VOCATIONAL TRAINING   Training practice before the 1960s was largely ad hoc; there was no sense that training could be a central part of corporate planning or strategy. Concern about the adequacy of Britain's training provision led to government intervention, in the form of the Industrial Training Act in 1964. The main aims of the Act were:

- to enable decisions on the scale of training to be better related to economic needs and technological development;
- to improve the overall quality of industrial training and to establish minimum standards;
- to enable the cost to be more evenly spread.

Industrial training boards (ITBs) were established – 27 by 1972 – with the statutory authority to operate a levy/grant system on employers. Under this scheme a levy was imposed on all employers within the industry and grants paid out to those achieving acceptable training. The process was discredited because of a range of factors, including:

- duplication of effort (between boards);
- overcentralization of the ITBs;
- bias towards the cultures and processes of the larger organizations;
- organizations merely trained to maximize levy rather than for motives centred on maximizing employee contribution to organizational goals;

● overbureaucratization of the ITBs.

The only training board now in existence is the Construction Industry Training Board (CITB). It has survived because it has been argued that the construction industry is a national industry and because of the itinerant nature of the workforce its training requirements can only be defined satisfactorily on a national basis.

The major activity of the CITB is concerned with Construction National Vocational Qualifications, levels 1, 2 and 3, and ensuring an adequate supply of trained craft labour. Lately this has been increasingly difficult to plan for, because of fluctuating economic activity, together with training problems caused by self-employment and labour-only subcontractors, a trend which is not likely to decrease.

MANAGEMENT TRAINING The model for most of the training activity in built environment organizations is based on a systems approach attributed to Boydell by Taylor.[12] The approach is highly systematic and involves isolating the learning required, setting objectives, designing the learning event, implementation, evaluation and feedback. In an examination of this systematic training model, Taylor [13] notes three underlying assumptions:

1. Training is seen as an investment for the organization.
2. Allocation of resources to training is on the same basis as any other business area.
3. There is a high degree of mutuality of interests between the organization and the individual.

The important assumption that training is seen as an investment for the organization implies:

● 'that training is an investment by the organization in its human resources;
● that training competes with non-training initiatives for the solution of organizational problems or the taking of opportunities;
● that decisions about training are taken by the organization.'[13]

A challenge to this assumption came in the conclusion of a report prepared in 1985 by Coopers and Lybrand Associates:

Few employers think training sufficiently central to their business for it to be a main component in their corporate strategy; the great majority did not see it as an issue of major importance . . . training (was) rarely seen as an investment but rather as an overhead which would be cut when profits are under pressure or as something forced on the company as a reaction to other developments.[14]

Thus training may be regarded as a cost to be minimized in times of crisis.

The second suggestion (that allocation of resources to training is on the same basis as any other business area) assumes that the current training issues are known and that an environment exists where an analytical appraisal can be made to formulate clear objectives. In reality, Taylor writes, training may be a form of organizational consumption which absorbs 'organization slack'; and he suggests that, where organizations are able to devote resources to training, this may have as much to do with an organization's domination of its respective markets, stable environments, technological advantage or stage protection as it has to do with 'enlightened management'.

The third statement (that the systematic training model assumes a high degree of mutuality between the interests of the organization and the needs of the individual) may accord with current thinking in terms of HRM but clearly this assumption cannot go unquestioned. For example, Taylor considers that training is often used at an individual level as a reward mechanism for good performance, 'which is a long way from the notion of providing training that is seen as contributing to the achievement of organizational objectives in a direct and rationally economic way.'[13]

In the context of built environment organizations, the major criticism of the systematic training model is that in order for it to be successful, it assumes a stable business environment where strategic planning is possible. As stated earlier, this is not a feature of many built environment organizations.

APPRAISAL

Appraisal is an important way of improving performance by establishing individual objectives. Provided that it is carried out accurately and fairly, it forms a link with reward and development.

WHAT IS MEASURED? Cummings and Scott[15] describe appraisals as having two broad purposes: an evaluative function, concerned with reviewing past performance, and a development function which concentrates on improving performance by identifying areas for improvement, setting performance targets and agreeing plans for follow-up action.

PERFORMANCE RATING   Logically, before a rating can be given a performance criteria needs to be agreed. Fletcher and Williams[16] suggest that a method such as job analysis should be used to identify specific performance criteria. They identify three broad categories into which these criteria fall:

- job or task oriented, emphasizing work outcomes or activities;
- worker oriented, emphasizing the behaviour of the job holder;
- abilities oriented, focusing on the underlying abilities or aptitudes required to perform the job.

WHO IS APPRAISED AND HOW OFTEN?   The most common practice is for the appraisal to be carried out annually by the immediate supervisor because, 'through close working contact and through guiding and controlling employees' activities, (the supervisor) is in a better position than anyone else to evaluate the employee's performance, strengths and weaknesses and training and development needs relating to the current job'.[17]

Fletcher and Williams[16] suggest that, in the site-based situation, the frequency of the job review could be increased and that more than one reviewer could be involved. Needless to say this would demand a considerable amount of coordination and staff time.

THE ROLE OF SELF-ASSESSMENT IN THE APPRAISAL
Studies show that the more the employee participates in the appraisal process the more satisfied he or she is likely to be with the appraisal interview and the appraiser, and the more likely it is that performance improvements will result.[18]

Fletcher and Williams[16] write that participation is meaningful 'when there is a genuine response from the appraiser – that is a willingness to listen and to act on the subordinate's ideas'. This requires an open and non-threatening organizational culture.

THE LINK WITH SALARY MANAGEMENT   The 'traditional British approach'[17] has 'separated' performance appraisal from pay decisions, the rationale being that conflict can arise between the objective of appraising performance and development and assessment of pay, using the same process. Other problems stem from the team-focused nature of the business, which raises issues about job design.

> Unless jobs are designed in ways to allow individual performance to be clearly assessed, it will be difficult to create an effective linkage to pay decisions.[16]

PERSONNEL MANAGEMENT AND EUROPE

Employment and social affairs have been a key aspect of the European Union, a concern which is articulated in the Social Charter or, using its official title, the 'Community Charter of the Fundamental Social Rights of Workers', which was adopted by all member states except the UK in December 1989. The charter is a Declaration and therefore has no legal force in itself. The intention behind the charter is that it should set a floor for basic common employment rights and objectives.

The charter emphasizes that these 12 principles would lead to a more effective use of human resources across the EU and therefore improve economic competitiveness and job creation. The UK is concerned that it would lead to costly and restrictive regulations which could damage competition.

GENERAL IMPACT OF THE EU ON PERSONNEL

RECRUITMENT The movement of labour is enshrined in the concept of the Single European Market. Employers may recruit throughout the EU and employees may work in any member state without a work permit, to enable employers to look beyond their national boundaries to find the best candidates for their vacancies and develop a 'European' workforce.

The immediate prognosis, however, is that mass movements of labour are not expected as a result of the consolidation of the Single European Market, but because of demographic trends leading to a shortage of young workers across the EU it is expected that certain categories of staff, especially senior managers, graduates and technical/specialist staff, will become more mobile as the supply of such personnel decreases.[18]

TRAINING Companies working in Europe need to ensure that certain employees are adequately trained in other langugages and in cultural awareness. Skills such as selling also need adapting to different markets, together with acquiring new knowledge of technical standards and rules.

Torrington[1] describes five stages in the historical development of personnel management. The current debate focuses upon real or apparent differences between personnel management and human resource management (HRM).

Three major differences are identified:

- In personnel management models, specialist personnel work is usually shown as added to the responsibilities of the manager, whereas such work is seen as an intrinsic part of the line management role.
- HRM is a bottom-up approach focusing upon employee development, whereas personnel management tends to be viewed from above and practised on subordinates.
- HRM models put a greater emphasis on the management of the organizational culture and identify a central activity for senior management.

This chapter describes the key processes of recruitment and selection; it also considers the induction of new staff and approaches to training and appraisal.

- What are the five stages of historical development of personnel management identified by Torrington[1]?
- What is meant by 'personnel management'?
- What is meant by 'human resource management'?
- What are the major differences between personnel management and human resource management?
- What are the two main personnel functions?
- What factors would you consider in devising a recruitment strategy?
- What selection methods might you use in recruiting new staff?
- What are the four main elements of a structured interview for a job?
- What is an appraisal criteria? How might your performance be assessed and measured?

1. Torrington, D. (1993) Human resource management and the personnel function, in *New Perspectives on Human Resource Management* (ed. J. Storey), Routledge, Chapter 4.

2.   Bain, G. (ed.) (1985) *Industrial Relations in Britain*, Blackwell.

3.   Fryer, G. (1990) *The Practice of Construction Management*, Professional Books.

4.   Torrington, D. and Hall, L. (1991) *Personnel Management, a new approach*, Prentice Hall.

5.   Guest, D. (1982) Human resource management and industrial relations. *Journal of Management Studies*, vol. 14, no. 10.

6.   Storey, J. (ed.) (1993) *New Perspectives on Human Resource Management*, Routledge.

7.   Guest, D. (1989) Personnel and human resource management – can you tell the difference? *Personnel Management*, Institute of Personnel Management.

8.   Hilebrant, P.M. and Cannon, J. (1990) *The Modern Construction Firm*, Macmillan.

9.   Robinson, I.T., Smith, M. and Copper, D. (1992) *Motivation, Strategies, Theory and Practice*, Institute of Personnel Management.

10. Sissons, K. (ed.) (1993) *Personnel Management in Britain*, Blackwell.

11. Fowler, A. (1991) How to conduct interviews effectively. *Personnel Management*, Institute of Personnel Management.

12. Taylor, H. (1991) The systematic training model: Corn circles in search of a spaceship? *Management Education and Development*, vol. 22.

13. Taylor, H. (1991) *Systematic Training Manual*.

14. Coopers and Lybrand Associates (1985) *A Challenge to Complacency: Changing attitude to training*, Manpower Services Commission.

15. Cummings, E.C. and Scott, W.E. (1973) *Readings in Organizational Behaviour and Human Performance*, Irwin.

16. Fletcher, C. and Williams, R. (1985) *Performance Appraisal and Career Development*, Hutchinson.

17. Anderson, G.C. (1993) *Managing Performance Appraisal Systems*, Blackwell.

18. Institute of Personnel Management (1994) *Personnel Management and Europe*.

MANAGEMENT DEVELOPMENT AND PERSONAL DEVELOPMENT

GRAHAM DARBYSHIRE

Management development is concerned with ensuring that an organization has the quantity and quality of managers it needs to meet its current objectives and strategic goals, the latter generally being the prime focus. Although larger organizations will require more complex processes to manage their management development activity, the principles of good practice and the core disciplines required will remain much the same, regardless of size.

Personal development is the development of an individual. It is seen from the point of view of the individual's needs and aspirations. Figure 10.1 illustrates the relationship between management development and personal development. Inevitably, the needs of the organization and of the employee will not always coincide. Furthermore, it is to be expected that many people will work for a variety of organizations during their careers, and prime responsibility for personal development must be retained by the individuals themselves. 'Delegating' responsibility to an employer is no longer a wise or realistic way for an individual to approach the process of personal development.

OBJECTIVES

After reading this chapter you should be able to:

● identify future management needs and requirements within an organization;

● understand the relationship between the culture of an organization and its impact on long-term goals;

● prepare training and development plans to meet the needs of these requirements both for the organization and personally.

INTRODUCTION

Figure 10.1   Management development and personal development.

THE MANAGEMENT DEVELOPMENT FRAMEWORK

Effective management development requires six elements to be carefully addressed in turn:

● Identification of the organization's future management needs at the macro level and how these will differ from the present. Within this, taking a 3- to 5-year view, there are three key questions:
  – What do we expect the organization to look like (structure, size and geography)?
  – How many managers at various levels do we expect to need? At the very least, will we need more or fewer?
  – How will the jobs of managers differ from the present?
● An appreciation of the organization's culture and the impact this will have on the declared longer-term goals.
● Identification of the more detailed management requirements, in terms of attitudes, skills and knowledge.

- Evaluation of how closely the existing management team meets the future requirements in terms of numbers, attitudes, skills and knowledge.
- Preparation of training and development plans which meet the needs arising from the above analysis.
- A review process.

Personal development planning is an approach by which individuals attempt to take more control over their lives through planned intervention. This chapter discusses the following issues:

- Should we make plans?
- Where are we now?
- Where do we want to be?
- How do we get there?
- Continuous Professional Development (CPD).

Two points need to be borne in mind when carrying out the above:

- Predicting the future is an imperfect science, but an honest, structured attempt to identify probable, or even possible requirements will always be better than flying blind.
- Any plan, however carefully prepared, must be kept under continual review, and adapted to meet the inevitable changes and unexpected situations that will arise. The plan will give focus and direction, but must never become a strait-jacket.

Subsequent sections deal with each of these subjects in more detail.

This can broadly be termed 'management manpower planning'. Firstly, the prime objective of an organization's management development activity must be to serve its future needs. To begin to identify those needs, the first place to look is the Strategic Plan. This will help to answer questions relating to projected size, activities, market share, market position, quality, services or products, territory and financial performance and, in particular, the question: 'Where does the organization want to be in 5 years' time?'

The second major consideration is the likely impact of external factors outside the organization's control on the employment of managers. For example:

PERSONAL DEVELOPMENT

IDENTIFICATION OF THE ORGANIZATION'S FUTURE MANAGEMENT NEEDS AT THE MACRO LEVEL

- demographic trends;
- likely availability of specialist skills;
- technological developments;
- social changes and attitudes to work;
- legal requirements;
- trends in employment practice;
- competitive forces.

Thirdly, what internal factors are directly relevant? For example:

- the age profile of the management team;
- under- or over-supply of managers at certain levels;
- the educational level of managers;
- the suitability of the current organization structure to meet future goals.

From the above analysis, it will be possible to answer more effectively certain key questions, such as:

- Is the structure and size of the organization expected to change radically?
- Will the number of management layers change?
- Will the number of managers required change significantly?
- Will the nature of management jobs change – for example, through the introduction of new technology, markets, management policies or employee expectations?
- Will it be more or less easy to attract and retain high calibre managers?
- Will there be a need to recruit a significant number of additional managers?

Whether an organization employs 50 or 50 000 people, the need to evaluate its likely future requirements is equally important. A professional practice with, say, 10 partners and 50 staff, where five partners are in their mid-50s, has just as great a need to plan for the future as a conglomerate with thousands of managers.

AN APPRECIATION OF THE ORGANIZATION'S CULTURE

There is not space in this chapter to dwell in depth on the question of culture. However, it remains vitally important that an organization understands its own culture and the type of manager and managerial behaviour that its culture fosters and encourages. For example, an organization which is risk-averse and autocratic, that emphasizes the achievement of short-term goals and discourages individuality, will have difficulty in developing an entrepreneurial culture, or increasing the level of 'empowerment' of staff, or introducing a decentralized organization structure in which managers are given high levels of local autonomy.

Cultures develop over many years and no organization can hope to change its culture quickly. But if the Strategic Plan calls for radical change and, for example, a new style of management, this will need to be taken carefully into account when the management development needs of the organization are being considered. In fact, it will directly shape the competencies and selection criteria of managers in the future.

If a significant cultural shift is to be achieved over a period of years, then comprehensive training will have to be undertaken across the organization to equip managers to adapt effectively to the new requirements, over and above any individual training needs which managers may have.

The identification of the organization's future management needs will have specified requirements at the macro level. It will not have determined whether or not members of the existing management team are competent or adequately equipped to meet those future needs and, if not, what needs to be done to close the gap. This poses two questions:

IDENTIFICATION OF MORE DETAILED MANAGEMENT NEEDS

● What precisely are the skills and knowledge that managers will require?
● Who possesses them, and to what extent, or who can be trained to possess them?

This section deals with the first question.

An increasing number of organizations use 'competencies' to help them with this process, although there is considerable debate on the definition and design of competencies, and equal variety in their application. Simply put, however, a **competency** can be defined as the set of attitudes, skills and knowledge which a person needs in order to perform a particular job to a competent standard.

COMPETENCIES

Typically, competencies are divided into three types:

● technical

- behavioural
- biographical.

Their application is in analysing and understanding job requirements more precisely than would be the case by taking a broad-brush approach.

The following descriptions serve to demonstrate what is meant by each type of competency:

- Technical competencies – the skills and knowledge which a job-holder requires to perform the job competently.
- Behavioural competencies – what a job-holder needs to be able to do through the application of the technical competencies.
- Biographical competencies – any physical, personal or practical requirements which are essential for competent performance. (These will usually be far fewer in number than the other two types of competency.)

To illustrate the difference between technical, behavioural and biographical competencies, let us take the example of a sales executive.

Technical competencies would include:

- product knowledge;
- call planning techniques;
- customer knowledge;
- knowledge of sales techniques.

Behavioural competencies would include:

- self-motivation;
- initiative;
- communications;
- judgement;
- adaptability.

Biographical competencies might include:

- holding a current clean driving licence;
- ability to travel and work overseas.

The technical and behavioural competencies listed above are merely the headings. Under each heading it would be necessary to describe, in one or two short sentences, the specific requirements of each competency.

The design of competency sets for jobs can be a hugely time-consuming and rigorous process. In larger organizations, where there may be dozens or even hundreds of people all doing similar management jobs, a major investment in time to produce high-quality competency sets will be justified due to the economies of scale. A more pragmatic approach is required in smaller organizations, which may have only 10 or 20 mangement jobs, each of which is different. Even in smaller organizations, however, a reasonable degree of analysis and care in producing competency sets will ensure that subsequent management development action is based on firm foundations. There is, quite simply, no point in embarking on expensive development activity if the general and specific objectives have not been properly identified.

Competencies help organizations to define what is required more precisely, and support many key processes within management development, in particular:

THE DESIGN AND APPLICATION OF COMPETENCIES

- Selection:
    - external recruitment;
    - internal recruitment.
- Performance appraisal.
- Training:
    - analysis of training needs;
    - training course design;
    - selection of external courses;
    - focus for on-the-job coaching.
- Assessment of future potential:
    - for different jobs at the same level;
    - for promotion;
    - preparation of individual development plans;
    - career planning;
    - succession planning: identifying an organization's ability to fill possible future vacancies from existing resources.

Whereas the technical competencies required by any managerial job will tend to be job-specific, behavioural competencies can often apply commonly to any one level of management, thereby simplifying their preparation. Generally speaking, the further a manager progresses up the organization, the greater will be the emphasis on behavioural competencies and the more important it will be to distinguish the behavioural competencies required at various levels. For example, middle, senior and general managers will all require the competency of 'leadership', but the definition of that competency will not be the same for a middle manager – with, say, 10 staff – as for a general manager, who may have several hundred staff.

The matrix in Figure 10.2 illustrates how the emphasis in jobs changes with promotion. A great deal of management development activity is focused on understanding these changes and on selecting and preparing people to cope with them effectively.

Level	Role
Middle management	Focus on operational issues. Managing people, processes and resources to achieve given objectives in a shorter time-scale.
Senior management	Developing systems and processes to implement strategic objectives. Managing through subordinate managers, usually covering a variety of specialist areas. Results measurable over a longer time-scale.
General management	Helping to develop strategy and shape strategic objectives. Creating structures and processes to achieve strategic objectives. Managing through senior managers, usually in a multi-disciplinary situation. Results usually measurable over 1 or more years.
Board	Accountable directly to shareholders. Shaping the role, goals and strategy of the organization. Managing through senior or general managers, invariably in a multi-disciplinary situation and often without detailed experience of many areas under their control. Results measurable over 1 to 3 years.

Figure 10.2 Differences in management level.

It would be typical for the behavioural competencies in a managerial job to cover 10–12 different headings, which might include visioning, communication, leadership, planning and control, commercial judgement, analysis, environmental awareness, decision making and political awareness. Figure 10.3 illustrates how a heading (in this case, 'Communication with staff') will differ in its detailed meaning from one level of management to another.

This section has aimed to illustrate what competencies look like and how they help in the analysis of the required skills and knowledge and their application. The next section focuses on how the competencies are used in practice to identify those managers who possess the required competencies or who can be developed to acquire them.

Middle Manager	Senior Manager	General Manager
Communicates in a clear, relevant and timely manner to staff, both orally and in writing.	Establishes effective communication processes within the function and regularly tests their effectiveness.	Determines the communication style and standards expected within the division.
Operates effective two-way communication processes.	Ensures that corporate strategy and objectives are understood and accepted by managers.	Defines the process required and ensures that senior managers establish and operate them.
Ensures that work objectives are clearly understood and feedback is given regularly.	Communicates commitment and enthusiasm for corporate goals.	Communicates corporate goals and vision in an impactful and motivating manner.
		Ensures that the communication process actively supports the achievement of corporate goals.

Figure 10.3 Behavioural competency: communication with staff.

There are several processes and techniques which organizations can use to evaluate the competence of their managers and to assess their potential to meet future needs. These processes and techniques, which are most effective when used in conjunction with competency sets, include:

● performance appraisal;
● psychometric testing;
● competency-based interviews;
● assessment centres.

Performance appraisal is concerned with performance in the current job and, as the competencies required in more senior jobs will differ, is not of direct benefit in predicting future potential.

Most commonly, performance appraisal schemes have the following features:

● They review performance against work objectives set at the beginning of the year or review period.

- They also review progress against any personal development objectives which may have been set; for example, to improve with respect to one or more particular competencies.
- They are two-way; that is, both the appraisal and appraiser (usually the immediate manager) participate in a discussion and exchange of views.
- They are used to identify training needs for the current job.
- They may be used to discuss other relevant issues; for example, the manager's management style, departmental problems, and so on.
- The results are usually recorded on a standard company form.
- The process often links into the setting of new work and personal development objectives for the coming year or review period.
- They often result in a performance rating, either against each objective set or against overall performance, or both.
- In many organizations they link directly or indirectly to salary or bonus payments, but this should never be their prime function, which should always be related to the effectiveness of the person in their job.

For management development purposes, predicting potential is even more important than reviewing current performance. The difficulty lies in that, by definition, it is difficult to predict how a person will perform in a situation that they have never previously experienced and for which there is therefore no evidence of ability on which to base judgements. By linking competencies to the three other processes listed above (psychometric testing, competency-based interviews and assessment centres) organizations can focus their predictive processes on the competencies that they know will be required in more senior positions.

PSYCHOMETRIC TESTING

Psychometric testing takes a variety of forms but should be carried out only by trained staff. It is best used in conjunction with other processes, such as competency-based interviews, or as part of an assessment centre. Tests come in two basic forms: aptitude tests and personality questionnaires.

Aptitude tests have been designed to measure a wide range of practical and intellectual abilities (the 11-plus exam is an example) and produce a score. This score can frequently be compared against national norms for various categories of staff.

Personality questionnaires do not measure ability but they record personal preferences, either at work or in a general context. They can also, for example, be used to identify the way in which a person prefers to operate in a team situation. These questionnaires do not result in any score being produced, but they do produce a 'profile' which will serve to indicate how a person will naturally respond in any given situation. 16PF and OPQ are examples of such questionnaires.

In these structured interviews, aimed at obtaining information about a person's competencies, questions are primarily of two types:

COMPETENCY-BASED INTERVIEWS

- 'When you have been in such-and-such a situation, what have you done?'
- 'If you were in such-and-such a situation, what would you do?'

The former type of question probes actual experience; the latter asks how a person would expect to perform in a situation which they have not actually experienced.

In the hands of a skilled interviewer, competency-based interviews can yield a great deal of valid information.

Both psychometric testing and competency-based interviews can be linked with evidence of a person's actual track-record (provided that this is relevant and linked to future competency requirements) to form a composite of relevant and objective information.

Many organizations have what are most commonly known as assessment centres. Although these can be powerful tools, they run a number of risks. They may be seen as threatening to those who undergo them and they can also cause individuals who perform less well than they had hoped to feel that they have 'failed' or that their careers will be blighted as a result of a few days' poor performance. Equally, people who perform well often develop exaggerated or unrealistic expectations of the speed and extent to which their careers will develop as a result. Assessment centres therefore need to be expertly designed and run. They also need to be the subject of thorough briefings to all involved, to be sensitively handled and to result in open, honest and constructive feedback.

ASSESSMENT CENTRES

The role of an assessment centre is to create simulated management situations which are observed by a number of observers or assessors, usually more senior managers within the organization. Tasks are so designed as to call for specific competencies – for example, those required in more senior jobs – if they are to be successfully completed. Such tasks include:

- presentations to a group;
- problem analysis;
- group discussion;
- planning exercises;
- 'in-tray' exercises;
- team exercises.

The performance of these tasks will normally be accompanied by one or more competency-based interviews and a number of psychometric tests, covering both aptitude and personality. By carefully evaluating the 'evidence' produced by this overall process – often carried out over a period of one, two or even three days – it is possible to make much more valid predictions of a manager's ability to perform in a future unfamiliar role.

Assessment centres have been used by employers for many years in the graduate recruitment process, when a student's intellectual ability and experience to date will provide limited evidence of the ability to perform in a very different working environment.

By using such processes, organizations can go a long way towards reducing the influence of personal bias, guesswork and subjectivity, and towards eliminating serious errors in the promotion of managers.

PERSONAL DEVELOPMENT

SHOULD WE MAKE PLANS?

Over the span of our working lives we may see radical changes in the relationships between the professional areas in the built environment. We may also find the general nature of employment changing with it becoming less likely that we remain in one job, or even one career, for life. One way of responding to such changes is to try to remain flexible and adaptable and to update our knowledge and skills progressively. Professionals and managers in the built environment, who spend much of their time planning and organizing for others, may have little time to plan for themselves. However, we are each responsible for ourselves and in that sense it could be said that we owe it to ourselves to plan and promote our own development.

We are all born with inherent qualities. Our lives and the way we develop are shaped and influenced by events, experiences and opportunities. As we reflect on our development there will be times when we see our own hand doing the shaping and times when we can see others as playing the major role. At different times and in different circumstances in our lives we may see that our needs and preferences have changed. There will be times when we have felt secure in following the guidance and controls of others and times when we have felt frustration and impotence in the face of such control.

Personal development planning is an attempt to take more control over our lives through a planned intervention. How do you feel about what is happening to you now, and what part do you want to play in influencing your future? Do you feel the need to be more reactive or proactive; or does the balance of influence and control over your life feel about right?

Some people do not like the concept of personal development planning; they find concepts such as identifying aspirations and objectives and exploring ways of getting there to be too mechanistic an approach to life in general. Many prefer to see themselves as responding to events and opportunities as they unfold, without the burden of analysing how they might have got where they are, or planning where they want to be. If you feel that planning for personal development is not for you, it may nevertheless be worthwhile to have an understanding of the approach and to explore some of the following techniques from time to time.

It is helpful to view personal development as a three-staged process in which we ask ourselves:

AN APPROACH TO PERSONAL DEVELOPMENT

- Where are we now?
- Where do we want to be?
- How do we get there?

WHERE ARE WE NOW?   Self-knowledge is the key to personal development. Understanding what we are and where we have been will give us a better chance of bringing into focus where we want to be and will provide clues as to how we might get there. Introspection, however, is not always an easy process. Workpieces 10.1–10.6 have been designed to help you to reflect upon your past by asking yourself, for example, how and why you came to choose the career path you are now following, what personal values were important in that choice, what strengths and weaknesses you have and how effective you are as a manager.

Please do not read any further until you have done Workpieces 10.1 to 10.4.

WORKPIECE 10.1

WHY AM I WHAT I AM?

In reading this book it is likely that you have decided to follow a career in the built environment. How did you come to this decision? What factors do you think were influential in choosing such a path? Was there one critical point or time at which you decided that this is what you wanted to do? Or was it an idea that grew over time?

Make brief notes on the following:

● How did the decision to follow your particular career come about?
● What were your reasons for choosing this career?
● What factors, events or people influenced your decision?

WORKPIECE 10.2

VALUES AND PERSONAL OBJECTIVES IN CAREER CHOICE

Look back again to the period in which you were coming to a decision about your future career. Consider the following 12 statements relating to goals, life values, personal objectives and achievements. Rank the statements from 1 to 12, in the order of how you may have seen their importance then.

● To be liked.
● To earn a great deal of money.
● To serve other people.
● To have a good time.
● To achieve a secure and stable position.
● To become an expert and an authority on a special subject.
● To become well known and obtain prestige, recognition and status.

● To be independent and to have the opportunity for freedom of thought and action.
● To make the most of your talents and achieve full personal development.
● To have a sense of duty and to be dedicated totally to the pursuit of ultimate values and principles.
● To be an influential leader and to organize and control others.
● To achieve something worthwhile.

If you decided upon a career path some time ago, rank these statements again in terms of how you see their importance to you now. Consider any changes that have taken place. What does this tell you about yourself?[2]

HOW I SEE MYSELF

Whilst we all have images of ourselves, they are not always easy to bring into focus. In order to clarify this picture construct a series of statements about yourself which would give someone else an idea of what you are like.[2]

Write 10 statements describing yourself beginning with the personal pronoun 'I':

'I ....'   'I ....'

'I ....'   'I ....'

'I ....'   'I ....'

'I ....'   'I ....'

'I ....'   'I ....'

WHAT ARE MY STRENGTHS?

What strengths do you think you have? You may have many qualities, but do you know what they are?[2] Complete 10 statements beginning with the phrase 'I am good at...':

'I am good at ....'   'I am good at ....'

'I am good at ....'   'I am good at ....'

'I am good at ....'   'I am good at ....'

'I am good at ....'   'I am good at ....'

'I am good at ....'   'I am good at ....'

Do not be surprised if you have to slow down to think after the first four or five statements in Workpiece 10.4. Many people do. Most of us are not accustomed to thinking of ourselves in this positive way. We may be more familiar with the negative view of finding faults and weaknesses (Workpiece 10.5).

Further insights into our strengths can often be obtained by asking others how they see us. Such an approach is not undertaken without personal risk and some people may find it too difficult. Many organizations in the built environment have introduced schemes for appraisal or performance review. Whilst these are often limited to assessing performance

WORKPIECE 10.5

WHAT ARE MY WEAKNESSES?

What do you see as your weaknesses? There will be things that you feel you should be able to do but cannot do, or perhaps cannot do very well. In addition there may be things you would like to stop doing.

I would like to do these things better:

I would like to begin to do these things:

I would like to decrease or stop doing these things:

against organizational targets, there may be useful personal development outcomes pointing to areas of needs. Yet another approach would be to use psychometric tests. In general it is best to draw on as many different methods as possible.

COMPETENCIES AND QUALITIES OF AN EFFECTIVE MANAGER   Thus far in exploring where we are now, we have been looking at strengths, weaknesses and values in broad general terms. Workpiece 10.6 brings a management perspective to this exploration, by focusing on specific management skills and qualities. Pedler, Burgoyne and Boydell[1] have suggested that effective managers possess 11 competencies:

- the ability to manage themselves;
- clear personal values;
- clear personal objectives;
- an emphasis on continuing personal growth;
- effective problem-solving skills;
- the capacity to be creative and innovative;
- the capacity to influence others;
- insight into management style;
- supervisory competence;

- the ability to train and develop others;
- the capability to form and develop effective teams.

Pedler *et al.*[1] argue that everyone has areas in which their competencies are underdeveloped. They describe a lack of skill or ability in any one of these areas as a 'blockage' and they recommend that 'the fastest and most economical way to bring about rapid self-development is to explore, understand and overcome these blockages, as they inhibit one's success and personal growth'. They suggest that managers who are competent in all these areas are likely to possess the following qualities:

- command of basic facts;
- relevant professional knowledge;
- continuing sensitivity to events;
- problem-solving, analytical and decision-/judgement-making skills;
- social skills and abilities;
- emotional resilience;
- proactivity – inclination to respond purposefully to events;
- creativity;
- mental agility;
- balanced learning habits and skills;
- self-knowledge.

WORKPIECE 10.6

THE EFFECTIVE MANAGER

Look back at your attempts to explore strengths and weaknesses in Workpieces 10.4 and 10.5. Use the list of competencies and qualities of the effective manager as a framework to consider the extent of your knowledge, skills, qualities and experience. Try to place your competencies, or qualities, in rank order.

This list of competencies can only provide the bones of a framework within which to view your effectiveness as a manager. Whilst you will find that many of the areas are discussed in this book, you may need to consult specialist texts. A number of these texts provide self-testing exercises. The 'Critical Blockages Survey' produced by Pedler *et al.*[1] is a good example of this.

WHERE DO WE WANT TO BE? Past experience influences the way we think about and plan for the future. Our perceptions of what has happened in the past, and why, often act to narrow our horizons and limit our expectations. Whilst much of our useful learning comes from experience, there are times when it is helpful to question the lessons that we have learnt and to push back accepted boundaries by thinking the unthinkable.

WORKPIECE 10.7

CREATE A VISION OF YOUR FUTURE

1. Predict

   What can you reasonably predict will happen next year? Consider the year ahead and think about some of its main features in the following terms:

   ● What you are likely to be doing.
   ● What is likely to happen to you.

   Make a list of these features (aim for at least 10). They do not have to be work related.

2. Like

   Reconsider the year ahead, this time focusing upon what you would like to do and what you would like to happen to you. Whilst being more optimistic about how you see the year unfolding, keep your ideas within the bounds of what you think is possible and realistic. Make another list of the same, or different, features of the year as you would like it to be.

3. Dream

   Again consider the year ahead of you, but this time relax all constraints and try to envisage what you would ideally like to do, or would ideally like to happen to you. This is a 'dreamland' where anything is possible. Rebuild your list. Again it could include those features you have already listed, or entirely new ones.

Look at these three lists together. How great are the differences between next year as you would predict it and the year you would like it, or dream it, to be?

The purpose of Workpiece 10.7 is to practise pushing back the boundaries built on experience and to discover more about hidden aspirations. Whilst it may be difficult to predict with any certainty what will happen beyond the next year, it can be even more revealing to repeat this exercise with a longer time horizons of, say, 5 or 10 years.

WORKPIECE 10.8

INFLUENCING THE FUTURE

Consider each feature on your list headed 'Like' from Workpiece 10.7 and try to think of any action you could take to make it more likely to happen. Treat this as a brainstorming exercise (as described in Chapter 6) and go first for the quantity of ideas for action rather than quality.

Repeat this exercise using your list of 'Dream' features.

Exercises of this type occasionally throw up strange ideas. If this happens, do not discard them immediately as nonsense; they may be your ticket to dreamland!

HOW DO WE GET THERE?   The development plan for built environment professionals does not have to be confined to training programmes and academic courses. Once individuals have identified their specific development needs, the opportunities for meeting them become much wider. In employment they can actively seek out roles and tasks that meet these needs. For example, at work it may be possible to take advantage of opportunities to give presentations to different sizes and types of audience; to learn new software applications; to act in a training role with junior staff; to be a member of a selection panel, and so on. If you are in a job in which there is insufficient scope to gain the experience of skills that you have identified, it may be possible to agree periods of secondment to other areas of work. The extent to which you can find opportunities at work to meet your own assessment of development needs can become a useful bargaining factor in annual assessments and job interviews.

Sometimes it is not possible to find specific personal development opportunities in the workplace but there may be ways of gaining experience through voluntary activities such as working with a parish council, a parents–teachers association, or the committee of a housing association.

Our view of the future may change depending on how long a time-scale we consider. Whilst the range of possible options tends to increase with time, so does the level of uncertainty which surrounds them. It is useful therefore to take both a long view and a short view.

Take, for example, a built environment undergraduate who is looking in the long term towards a number of different goals including becoming a senior partner in a consultancy, a chief officer of a local authority, or perhaps running a private practice. In the shorter term the routes to all these goals might include some similar career steps and stages of professional development. It may be possible to visualize the first five years in some detail and even with a fair level of certainty. The common steps might be completing a degree course, starting a first job and reaching professional qualification. Within each of these stages there are many opportunities to make choices. For example, within a degree programme there may be choices about specialist units, and in

PREPARING A
PERSONAL
DEVELOPMENT PLAN

first employment there may be choices and decisions about what further training to undertake. For this individual, plans stretching beyond 5 years may be as yet fairly sketchy. However, with the vision of a goal (even if there are several visions and a number of different goals), this undergraduate is better placed to identify and evaluate opportunities as they arise.

A useful technique for personal development planning is to take time out from our normal routine and have a meeting with ourselves. This is similar to the approach of 'suspending business' which we advocated for new teams who are managing tasks. The idea of a 'meeting with ourselves' is to spend time working through a 'personal agenda'. The outcomes of such a meeting might be to take stock of where we are, reflect on the direction and progress we are making and re-examine our vision of the future. A personal development plan does not need to be highly detailed with fixed goals and deadlines. It is more of a continuous process by which we take stock and rebuild our perspectives in response to changes in circumstances and opportunities, and to changes in our own values and aspirations.[2]

WORKPIECE 10.9

A PERSONAL AGENDA

You have decided to prepare a personal development plan and as a first step to have a 'meeting with yourself'. What items would appear on your agenda?

WORKPIECE 10.10

PERSONAL DEVELOPMENT PLAN

Prepare a personal development plan. Use a time-scale that suits your circumstances.

- Identify personal goals in the short and long term.
- Look back to Workpiece 10.6 and identify specific

steps for skills building to address the weaknesses you have noted.
- Describe stages of career development which could reasonably lead you towards these goals.

CONTINUOUS PROFESSIONAL DEVELOPMENT (CPD)

Professional bodies in the built environment are increasingly requiring their members to update their skills, knowledge and expertise. A variety of continuous professional development (CPD) schemes have been put in place; some are compulsory, others voluntary. Institutions give their support and approval to programmes of training, conferences and activities to encourage their members to undertake CPD. By going through the three stages of personal development planning, professionals and managers would clearly put themselves in a much better position to build an effective CPD programme.

Management development is concerned with ensuring that an organization has the quantity and quality of managers it needs to meet both its current objectives and its strategic goals. Whether the organization employs 50 or 50 000 people, the need to evaluate its likely future requirements is equally important. Where a strategic plan calls for radical change, management development may involve programmes of comprehensive training to equip managers to adapt to those changes.

At the more detailed level, management development is concerned with identifying the skills and knowledge that individual managers require. Many organizations identify technical, behavioural and biographical competencies in analysing specific job requirements. These competencies are used to support the key management development processes of selection, performance appraisal, training and the assessment of future potential.

Predicting potential is often seen as more important than reviewing current performance. Some organizations go to considerable lengths to remove personal bias, guesswork and subjectivity from the selection process and make use of psychometric testing, competency-based interviews and assessment centres.

Personal development planning is an attempt to take more control over our lives through a planned process of intervention. There are typically three stages in which we ask: 'Where are we now?', 'Where do we want to be?' and 'How do we get there?'

Pedler *et al.*[1] recommend that the fastest and most economical way to bring about rapid self-development is to explore, understand and overcome 'blockages', as they inhibit one's success and personal growth. Once we have identified our development needs, the opportunities for meeting them become much wider as it is possible to seek out specific tasks and roles. A useful technique for personal development planning is to take time out and have a meeting with ourselves. The objective is to suspend our usual business and spend time working through a personal agenda.

A personal development plan does not need to be highly detailed with fixed goals and deadlines. It is more of a continuous process by which we take stock and rebuild our perspectives in response to change.

CHECKLIST OF POINTS

MANAGEMENT DEVELOPMENT

- What factors might you take into consideration when evaluating the management development needs of an organization?
- Why might cultural change in an organization give rise to the need for training?
- What is meant by technical, behavioural and biographical competencies?
- How does the emphasis on competencies tend to change as a manager progresses into the higher levels of an organization?
- What features would you generally expect to find in a performance appraisal scheme?

PERSONAL DEVELOPMENT

- Why should you plan your personal development?
- What is the key to personal development?
- What are the competencies and qualities of an effective manager?
- In what ways can you meet your specific development needs?

REFERENCES

1. Pedler, M.J., Burgoyne, J.G. and Boydell, T.H. (1978) *A Manager's Guide to Self-Development*, McGraw-Hill.
2. Manpower Services Commission (1987) *Management Self-Development*.

FURTHER READING

Bennett, R. (1989) *Personal Effectiveness*, Kegan Page.
Evans, D.E. (1986) *People, Communication and Organisation*, Pitman.
Evans, R. (1990) *The Creative Manager*, Unwin.
Francis, D. (1985) *Managing your own Career*, Fontana.
Pedler, M. and Boydell, T. (1988) *Managing Yourself*, Fontana.

INDEX

Also available from E & FN Spon

Brain Train
Studying for success
R. Palmer and C. Pope

Construction Contracts
Law and management
J.R. Murdoch and W. Hughes

Construction Methods and Planning
J.R. Illingworth

Economics
A foundation course for the built environment
J.E. Manser

Effective Writing
Improving scientific, technical and business communication
Second edition
C. Turk and J. Kirkman

The Idea of Building
Thought and action in the design and production of buildings
S. Groàk

Profitable Practice Management
For the construction professional
P. Barrett

Project Management Demystified
Today's tools and techniques
Second edition
G. Reiss

Risk Analysis in Project Management
J. Raftery

Value Management in Design and Construction
J. Kelly and S. Male

For more information on these and other titles published by E & FN Spon, please contact: *The Promotions Department, 2–6 Boundary Row, London, SE1 8HN. Telephone 0171 865 0066.*